UNTO THE HILLS

PSALM CXXI .

Levavi oculos.

DYRCHAFAF fy llygaid i'r mynyddoedd : o'r lle y daw fy nghymmorth.

2 Fy nghymmorth a ddaw oddi wrth yr Arglwydd : yr hwn a wnaeth nefoedd a daear.

3 Ni ad efe i'th droed lithro : ac ni huna dy geidwad.

4 Wele, ni huna : ac ni chwsg ceidwad Israel.

5 Yr Arglwydd yw dy geidwad : yr Arglwydd yw dy gysgod ar dy ddeheulaw.

6 Ni'th dery'r haul y dydd : na'r lleuad y nos.

7 Yr Arglwydd a'th geidw rhag pob drwg : efe a geidw dy enaid.

8 Yr Arglwydd a geidw dy fynediad, a'th ddyfodiad : o'r pryd hwn hyd yn dragywydd.

PSALM CXXI .

Levavi oculos.

I will lift up mine eyes unto the hills : from whence cometh my help.

2 My help cometh even from the Lord : who hath made heaven and earth.

3 He will not suffer thy foot to be moved : and he that keepeth thee will not sleep.

4 Behold he that keepeth Israel : shall neither slumber nor sleep.

5 The Lord himself is thy keeper : the Lord is thy defence upon thy right hand;

6 So that the sun shall not burn thee by day : neither the moon by night.

7 The Lord shall preserve thee from evil : yea, it is even he that shall keep thy soul.

8 The Lord shall preserve thy going out, and thy coming in : from this time forth for evermore.

UNTO THE HILLS

Hilda Hunter

BREWIN BOOKS

Cover photograph taken by the Author near Meirion Mill,
Dinas Mawddwy.

First Published by Brewin Books Ltd.,
Studley, Warwickshire 1998

British Library Cataloguing in Publication books.
A catalogue record for this book in available
from The British Library.

ISBN: 1 85858 120 6

Typeset in Plantin.
Printed by Warwick Printing Company Limited,
Theatre Street, Warwick, CV34 4DR

The Author

PREFACE

Dear Hilda,

This morning, I took up *Unto the Hills*, and found it so riveting that I finished it soon after noon: a *marvellous* read!

What a remarkable life you have had! beginning in the slow, quiet days of the year after the Great War ended, in Blackheath, Staffordshire (a town to which The Royal Automobile Club ascribes no population whatever, and which The Post Office has deleted as a postal address); which would mean little to most of us had you not sketched it so carefully; embedding your description both chronologically and geographically till we walk the lanes with you, and feel where the shoe pinches.

I say "where the shoe pinches" because it *did* pinch, did it not? When we see such places, and such times, on television and in film, it is the insufficiency of provision above all that strikes us, and which brings home to us how surprisingly well off most of us are now in comparison with those harsh days.

I loved "The Call of the Hills"! and your father sounds so like mine, even to insisting that everyone stand for the National Anthem in the middle of a meal. "A perfectionist is one who takes infinite pains, and gives them to others", eh? (Mind you, I share some of his obsessions; to such an extent that my wife, reading your pen-picture of him, said, "My word! isn't he like *you*!"). What a good-looking man he was in youth! as a woman was your mother.

Wasn't it strange that Stewarts & Lloyds would promote men who had not been to the Front, and hold back men who had? That brings out the difference in ethos between the Georgian era and our own in a way that reverses our expectations.

I was touched to read of Mary's ill-omened birth and unsuccessful operation for *strabismus;* and how cruelly and unnecessarily her precious diary was suppressed by the ill-starred Doris (it is rare for an autobiography to have a Wicked Witch of the West; but none the less welcome for all that).

It was helpful of you to show us Mr Parkes's actual letter concerning Mary's progress at school. Your outburst on page 37 of chapter three concerning Father's treatment of her was richly deserved, for all that it silenced Father at the time.

How fascinating it was that the two teachers at Stourbridge who most influenced you were the only beauties on the staff! (I wonder whether that had anything to do with their success?). The illustrations really do bring your story to life. What a sublimely *happy* company we see in "Forms VI Lower & Upper"!

I was struck by the advance in your powers of versification: particularly in its unusual rhyme-scheme: in "Summer 1937", whose topic is not unlike that of W H Auden in the same era. The detail of your description of telegraphy in chapter six reminded me of Dorothy L Sayers's *tour de force* in *The Nine Tailors*. What a noble face Lucy Vincent turns to the camera at Harlech in 1958 on p 112!

I envied your contact with so many really wise advisers. Frank Edwards's advice to "step in at the level you want to achieve" could have saved many a career from fizzling out; but, before doing so, you had to combine business-life and musical life in a way which cannot have been easy.

Now, to me, your story becomes mesmeric: partly because your early home-life had had so little music in it; partly because here you are, rubbing shoulders with so many musical people of national to international reputation: Sir Granville Bantock; Dr Walter Bergmann; Dr Alan Blackall; Dr Christopher Edmunds; Dr Ruth Gipps; Prof Anthony Lewis; Margaret Murray; Prof Ian Parrott; Prof J A Westrup, and Dr Percy M Young. What a change "from quiet homes and first beginnings"! and yet it was not all plain sailing, was it? when you discovered "laughter and the love of friends" in circles so distinguished.

The flowering, not only of talent, but of *personality* under your percipient guidance is instanced so remarkably in page after page on which we meet shy and faltering souls who become national figures, thanks to you, that we cannot but see you as one of the most successful teachers of the century; and this, to me, stems from perhaps your most unusual trait: that you asked advice (which is not all that common), and you acted on it (which is definitely uncommon); and, because you did, you were ready to do as you had been done by, and unhesitatingly to guide your students through the pitfalls and the sloughs of despond.

When I reached page 118, I thought, "Crikey! She's never going to leave Aberystwyth for Rowton Castle!" Your impending disaster stared me in the face before I even read of it; and this is the very stuff of drama. Thank *goodness* you didn't give up your car: but, then, your strength of mind and character shines from every page, no matter how turbulent the scenes through which we pass (not least, in flatly refusing to teach in unsuitable accommodation; or to continue in a post which was getting nowhere: not for you the hamster-treadmill which too many lack the enterprise to quit).

How good that you had so wise and unselfish an adviser in Prof Brodie Hughes! and what a picture of devotion you paint for us re the teacher at Berkeley in chapter ten!

The rounding off of your moving tale is just right; convincing us that you did, indeed, meet with triumph and disaster, and treat those two impostors just the same (you realize what *that* makes you, of course?). The balance and polish of your story make it immensely worth reading, and the sheer moral goodness in the faces that you show us help to carry us into an era, into circles and to places that too few of us have sampled.

What a privilege it has been to read your story!

Thank you.

CHARLES CLEALL
Warden, Education Section, Incorporated Society of Musicians,
1971-72

Northern Divisional music specialist of Her Majesty's Inspectorate
of Schools in Scotland, 1972-87

CONTENTS

Chapter 1:

ROOTS AND REBELS

If there was one dominant characteristic in our family, it was obstinacy. Perhaps obstinacy was a feature in the temperament of Black Country people in general – a trait essential to survival in lives fraught with difficulties and problems and lived out in a predominantly unattractive environment. Or perhaps ours was born and bred in the Yorkshire and Westmorland origins of my grandparents and their forbears.

There are many synonyms for the word obstinate. Some, for example tenacious, persistent, are more or less complimentary: others, such as headstrong, mulish, opinionated, perverse, pigheaded, are downright derogatory. I have been called all of these – so have members of our family – probably with justification!

My own recollections go back to the early 1920's, to life at home at 62 (later re-numbered as 63) Highfield Road, Blackheath, Birmingham. That was the original postal address, though Blackheath has never had any affinity with Birmingham or its people. It is in Staffordshire anyway. Its present-day postal address, dating from 1974, fails to include the word Blackheath at all; instead, Blackheath is apparently submerged in 'Rowley Regis, Warley, West Midlands'. Rowley Regis was originally a small village adjacent to Blackheath but with a separate identity. Warley lies some four miles east of Blackheath, with which it has little, if anything, in common. However, West Midlands indicates more accurately the present-day character of Blackheath as a somewhat undistinguished member of a large group of communities, each once unique, but now scarcely identifiable either geographically or culturally.

In the early part of the twentieth century (and undoubtedly earlier), each small community was physically separated from its neighbours by fields, or, where mining and industrial pollution had done their worst, by areas of derelict land. Transport links were sparse. Some of the places now known collectively as the West Midlands protested their independence from the Black Country, sited in their midst, which they generally regarded with some disdain as being socially and environmentally inferior.

This separation of communities resulted in the preservation of quite disparate dialects and speech characteristics for even the smallest communities.

Repairing overhead tramway cables in High Street, Blackheath
Postcard dated August 16th, 1904

For instance, not only were there differences between the dialects of Blackheath and Halesowen, places no more than two miles apart, but also between the dialects of each of those small towns and that of the intervening community of Gorsty Hill, which had developed a separate identity. Gorsty Hill speech was very guttural (except when mothers called their children in from the street in high-pitched and ear-splitting yells!); vowel sounds were distorted and ugly, and a majority of the people spoke in a dialect unintelligible outside the immediate vicinity.

Families in the areas of Halesowen, Blackheath and Gorsty Hill depended heavily on the local firm of Lloyd and Lloyd for employment, in Coombs Wood Steel Tube Works. The firm developed out of the project of a Mr. Barnsley who, in 1860, started a factory on a site of one acre. In 1870 the enterprise was taken over by two gentlemen both named Lloyd and the firm was known as Lloyd and Lloyd. In 1901 John Graham Stewart became Chairman of the Company and in 1903 it became Stewarts and Lloyds, Limited. The management had a strong Scottish element which predominated throughout the life of the firm, which expanded worldwide and acquired many subsidiaries. An important branch was established in the early 1930's at Corby, Northamptonshire, where a whole new town grew around the factory from a nucleus of volunteers drawn from Coombs Wood.

Coombs Wood was an area of land to the southeast of Gorsty Hill, but at a considerable depth below it. The curious contour of the area may have been due to coal extraction and consequent collapse. The entire factory – always known as 'the Works' – was in this deep hollow. The Works was about a mile long and of variable width, bisected lengthwise by a canal which provided transport facilities for raw materials and finished products. It had a private exterior road, closed on one day annually to confirm privacy, the Blackheath end of which was a very steep hill known as 'the Tip'.

Part way down the Tip was Coombs Wood School, attended by the infants of the area. The foundation stone was laid in 1897 by Mrs. Henry Howard, wife of one of the Directors of Lloyd and Lloyd. Next to the school was built St. Ambrose Mission, an offshoot of St. Paul's Church, Blackheath. It was named after its benefactor, Mr. Ambrose Lloyd, of the firm of Lloyd and Lloyd. Along the side of St. Ambrose Mission was a path, known locally as 'Lovers' Walk', running along the bank on the leeward side of the Works and just below the road known as 'Cocksheds'. The land beside the path was originally grass-covered, but it became barren, due to the effect of continuous smoke from the Works.

The Staff of Coombs Wood School c.1904
Back Row: Miss Annie Bennett, —, —, Mother (Miss Sarah Sidaway),
Front: —, Mr John Marshall (Headmaster), —.
(John Marshall's son became Office Manager of Stewarts and Lloyds Ltd.)

Every Saturday at midday, the chimney stacks were deliberately fired in order to clear them of debris, and thick black smoke enveloped the entire area.

Opposite the Works Gates and at the side of the Tip was a row of forty small terraced houses (including two small shops) known as 'the Building'. These had been built by the Firm, which rented them to employees. They were very basic indeed. Each had a very steep garden, rising to the level of Gorsty Hill. Flights of dangerously steep and uneven steps between blocks of houses provided access between the Works and Gorsty Hill.

The fact that the entire factory was considerably below the surrounding land levels contributed to its survival through the war of 1939-1945, when its vast expanse of roofing was camouflaged and it was rendered unidentifiable from the air, thus escaping the attention of German bombers.

In 1992, as a consequence of the the decline in the steel industry, Coombs Wood Works was closed and later demolished. This was a saddening event in the neighbourhood, in view of the honourable history of the Firm. For many families, the Works had represented not only a means of earning a living for several generations, but also a way of life based on mutual loyalties between employers and employees.

The Firm was heavily involved in the manufacture of munitions for both World Wars. An outstanding achievement during the second World War and described in detail in a book published by the Firm under the title "An Industrial War Record", was the design and manufacture of "Pluto". Here is a quotation from the book:

> "Pluto" stands for "Pipe Lines under the Ocean", and our work in connection with the project might be regarded as part of the multifarious uses to which our tube and pipe were put during the war. Our responsibility, however, went far beyond the supply of pipe, and in fact we became so deeply involved that it is only right to include "Pluto" within the sphere of our special war effort. The story has already been published and filmed and only the barest outline need be given here. The broad conception was to lay pipe lines to carry petrol under the English Channel and thereby link up the 1,000 miles of pipeline network that had been installed in England with the European pipelines that would follow the advances of the Allied Armies after D Day – in short, the transport of oil from a tanker in the Mersey to our troops on the Rhine by a continuous pipeline.

The book is well worth reading for its detailed text and provision of explanatory photographs, together with tributes paid by Churchill and Eisenhower to the

Firm's achievements. It also gives some idea of the enormous size and worldwide influence of Stewarts and Lloyds and its many subsidiaries.

My grandfather, Thomas Hunter, came south from Middlesborough, Yorkshire, in 1869, hoping to find work in the steel industry of the Black Country. He was employed by Lloyd and Lloyd, and took lodgings at the home of Martha Sidaway, my maternal grandmother, next door to 'The Anchor' public house. After the death of her husband (from developments arising from cancer of the lips, said to have been caused by his habitually smoking a clay pipe), Martha Sidaway moved to the 'Old Cot' in Lodgefield Road, Gorsty Hill. This was the last house before the cornfields.

Grandfather John Albert Sidaway and Grandmother Martha Sidaway, c.1910

Martha Sidaway had four daughters, of whom my mother was the youngest. She employed the owner of a local brickworks to build four terraced houses near to the 'Old Cot' so that each daughter would eventually have her own house. The block was called 'Mafeking Villas', since they were built in 1900, the year of the relief of the siege of Mafeking in the Boer War.

The four Sidaway sisters: Kezia, Elizabeth, Fanny and Sarah Martha, c.1900

Grandfather Thomas Hunter returned home to Middlesbrough and married Elizabeth Hartley in 1870. She came from Troutbeck in Westmorland, but little is known about her except that her great-grandmother was Margaret Longmire who lived to be 104! The sixth of their seven children was my father, William James Hartley Hunter. He was born in Middlesbrough on 6th January, 1883. The family left there in 1887 and came to live at 6, Coombs Wood Building.

On 13th April, 1910, William James Hartley Hunter was married to Sarah Martha Sidaway at Halesowen Parish Church.

My father, William James Hartley Hunter, c. 1900

William and Sarah were determined that any children they should have would be brought up away from the sound and influence of Gorsty Hill speech so that they might have a reasonable chance of a good start in life.

After their marriage, instead of going to live in Sarah's house in Mafeking Villas (as was expected of them), they rented a house on the western edge of Blackheath in Highfield Road. Their first baby – a boy – failed to survive. Subsequently they bore three daughters. My elder sister, Doris Muriel, was born on 2nd April, 1915. I followed on 6th December, 1919. Mary was born on 4th January, 1927.

My parents rented the house in Highfield Road for many years at seven shillings and sixpence weekly. In 1932, the landlord, Mr. William Cooper (then in his nineties), died. His properties were offered for sale and my parents bought the house for £250. My father at that time earned only two or three pounds weekly. In common with most families, my parents never bought anything for which they could not pay immediately; so the purchase of the house drained their resources – and this in a time of deep economic recession.

The name 'Blackheath' is said to be a corruption of 'Bleak Heath'. Highfield Road, on the edge of a ridge facing the prevailing winds from west and southwest, certainly bears this out. Doctor McQueen, who visited us in times of illness, used to say that it was a very healthy place to live in – if you could only survive it!

We were not in the path of the smoke from Stewarts and Lloyds, only ten minutes' walk away to the south and down in its hollow. But a southwest wind would blow sulphurous smoke from the steam trains entering and leaving the Rowley Tunnel (between Old Hill station and that of Rowley Regis and Blackheath) straight across to the back of our row of houses.

Our house was high above our back garden which was reached by descending nine steep stone steps. Below were the back gardens of houses in Perry Park Road, a long loop of road built to accommodate trams to and from Blackheath and Dudley via Old Hill and Netherton, which could not negotiate the more direct and much steeper incline of Waterfall Lane. The area contained within the loop was called 'The Tump'. It was rough hillocky land with a central flat patch, much used by boys for football and cricket. Sometimes a Wake would come there for a few days, with stalls and roundabouts. The railway tunnel between Old Hill Station and Rowley Regis and Blackheath Station began deep down in a cutting below the loop of Perry Park Road.

On one occasion, a circus came to the Tump. The lions in their cage must have become very restive; they toppled their cage which started to roll away. It went down the steeper side of the Tump, crossed Perry Park Road, broke through the rails at the top of the railway cutting and rolled down, coming to a halt on the railway lines! What happened afterwards I know not, but the lions must have been very shaken.

On the occasion of the Silver Jubilee of King George V and Queen Mary in 1935, and also on the occasion of the Coronation of King George VI and

Queen Elizabeth in 1937, celebratory bonfires, built on the Tump, could be seen for many miles around.

Above the railway tunnel was a rough grassy bank, presumably formed from earth excavated when the tunnel was constructed. Adjacent to the top of the bank was 'Highfields', a continuation of Highfield Road. In the 1920's part of this was a cornfield. Another part was grazed by cattle belonging to the local farmer, Mr. Sturman, whose house in Beeches Road had ducks on a pool in front of it. The land over the top of the mile-long tunnel was deemed too unstable for buildings to be erected on it, so the fields remained unspoilt for many years. Gradually houses were built where the fields had been, but the land directly over the tunnel remained rough and unused.

View from Highfields, looking towards Old Hill Station. The 'Rowley Tunnel' took GWR trains, via Rowley Regis and Blackheath Station, to Snow Hill Station, Birmingham. Perry Park Road is right of picture.

(Photograph taken by H. Hunter in early 1998)

Extremes of height and depth were common in our part of the Black Country. Some were natural in origin, but the landscape was also spectacularly affected by mining and subsidence. Also, as in the case of the Rowley Hills, a mile or so to the north of our house, ugly gashes resulting from the quarrying of granite ('Rowley Rag', used in road-making) were all too evident – though we appreciated the gradual replacement of 'dirt' roads by metalled surfaces! On the eastern side of Blackheath, towards Birmingham, these configurations of landscape did not appear and the land was much flatter. The flatter eastern side of the Black Country is separated from the hilly western side by the Rowley Hills, a part of the 'dorsal ridge'.

Though the Rowley Hills stood much higher than Highfield Road, we had a very extensive view from the yard at the back of our house. There would have been an even better one from the bedroom window but for the existence of an unbelievably wide and ugly expanse of red brick chimney with two enormous pots. It was built on top of the kitchen, about four feet from the bedroom window to take away smoke from the kitchen fire and from a non-existent boiler in the room underneath the kitchen at garden level, known as the 'Toolhouse'.

Our view westward was over Old Hill, Cradley Heath, Colley Gate, Lye and Stourbridge, to Kinver Edge, identifiable through binoculars. Beyond, on the horizon, we could see the Brown Clee and Titterstone Clee hills, some thirty miles away in Shropshire. Looking southwest we could see Halesowen – nothing to bar the view of the church spire in those days – and beyond, Hunnington, identified by the chimney of Harry Vincent's 'Bluebird' Toffee Factory.

Also to the southwest, in an arc of some four or five miles' radius we could see clearly the hills of Romsley, Walton, Clent and Hagley. From Highfields on a very clear day, the Malvern and Abberley Hills were visible. Rain came normally from the direction of Walton and Clent and we could observe its approach. On washing days, if the wind was not too strong, Mother would have time to gather the washing from the line in the garden before the rain reached us.

Northwestwards, we could see Netherton, Brierley Hill and Dudley, each with its distinctive church; Netherton and Brierley Hill Churches were identifiable by their square towers and Dudley 'Top' Church by its spire on the horizon. The factory of Marsh and Baxter, Brierley Hill (famous for its pork pies and sausages) was clearly visible on the skyline. So was 'The Earl of Dudley's Round Oak Steelworks' with its distinctive tall chimney stacks; after demolition, it was replaced by the 'Merry Hill Shopping Centre'. To our extreme right, looking northward, we could see, on a clear day, the top portion of the Wellington Wrekin, some thirty miles distant.

Sometimes we would walk the four or five miles from home to Walton or Clent Hill, from which we could see our panorama in reverse, with the added landmark of the University tower at Edgbaston, Birmingham.

In our part of the Black Country, therefore, we were always climbing or descending hills and rarely walking in flat places. This fact, coupled with the incredible views of the surrounding country, was possibly the origin of my lifelong fascination with places and maps and of my lust for travelling, whether on foot, scooter, bicycle, or – many years later – by car. I have always been unmoved by flat places, but obsessed with hills and mountains, not so much with a view to climbing them but to experience that peace of mind which is created by just being among them. Not surprisingly, my favourite among the Psalms has always been Psalm 121: "I will lift up mine eyes unto the hills, from whence cometh my help...."

This poem was written in 1935. I had asked if I might do my private study in the school garden on a warm sunny day in the Summer term. I was told that I might do so, on condition that I wrote a poem for the school magazine, 'The Pear Tree'!

THE CALL OF THE HILLS
(With apologies to Mr. Masefield).

I must go up to the hills again – to the hills at the dawn of day,
When the larks welcome the sunrise and the rabbits come out to play;
And the moon fades, as the sun's rays set sparkling the dewy ground,
While a cool breeze stirs the pine trees, where the cuckoo's notes resound.

I must go up to the hills again, where Nature is most fair,
And refreshed I climb in the morning's prime, and breathe the fresh
    spring air;
The stream and the wood I leave far below and climb toward the rising sun;
Soon I shall stand on the brow of the hill – the quest of my journey won.

H. HUNTER, VI Lower.

Chapter 2:

PURSUIT OF PERFECTION

My father left school in 1896 at the age of thirteen to become an office boy at Lloyd and Lloyd's, where his father and elder brother, Thomas, were already employed in engineering. Father was fascinated by engines and anything mechanical, and he was also keenly interested in English language and literature. He enrolled at the 'Centre' in Wright's Lane, Old Hill, to study mathematics, engineering drawing and Shakespeare.

Father requested a transfer from the Office to the Engineering Department, where he became a Fitter, eventually with responsibility for the maintenance of complex machinery. He worked as a Fitter for the remainder of his fifty-seven years' service with the Firm. In 1955, at the age of seventy-two, he was asked to take retirement. He did not enjoy the years which followed because, possibly due both to inactivity and lack of purpose, his health deteriorated. He died in 1967 at the age of eighty-four years.

Father was a total perfectionist. He could be extremely patient, especially in the solution of mechanical problems. He had a good memory, and his learning – though limited in scope – was thorough. His speech, writing and spelling were impeccable; he regarded poor writing as an inexcusable discourtesy because it wasted the time of those who had to struggle to read it. He was intolerant of imprecise speech and pedantic to the point of rudeness in correcting the faults made by others in conversation with him; he obstinately refused to continue a conversation until appropriate words were used. He was meticulous himself and demanded reciprocal precision from others.

Perfectionists are notoriously difficult to live with, in both workplace and home; Father was no exception. It was said that promotion eluded him on account of his uncompromising demand for perfection from others. His meticulous attention to detail and his dogged persistence in resolving difficulties were undoubtedly admired and respected by his employers, and also by a small minority of his fellow workers. However, he conspicuously failed to form easy working relationships, and many people saw him as proud and arrogant. He was not in the least gregarious and had very few friends: but he gave little encouragement to anyone who sought his friendship.

COOMBS WOOD WORKS
LONG SERVICE EMPLOYEES
(OVER 50 YEARS CONTINUOUS SERVICE)
— JANUARY 1950 —

1	FREDERICK BARNSLEY	12	SAMUEL PENNELL	23	PERCIVAL COLEY	34	WILLIAM PUGH (B FINISHING)	45	ABRAHAM SHERWOOD
2	G. FREDERICK BROOME	13	CALEB NOCK	24	ERNEST PAYNE	35	GEORGE LOWE	46	ANDREW HARRIS
3	ALBERT GREEN	14	CHARLES RUDGE	25	EDWIN BAYNHAM	36	JONATHAN BLUNT	47	ARTHUR CUTLER
4	JESSE HICKTON	15	FRANK ROBINSON	26	GEORGE TAYLOR	37	ALBERT WESTON	48	ALBERT REYNOLDS
5	WILLIAM LAYTON	16	ALBERT EDWARDS	27	WILLIAM TROMANS	38	ROBERT WHYLE	49	JOSEPH BAYNHAM
6	SAMUEL BISSELL	17	G. BERT SIVITER	28	THOMAS TURNER	39	PERCY RANKLE	50	FRANK DALLOW
7	CHARLES WILLIAMS	18	C.B. McNAIR (WORKS MANAGER)	29	MAJOR WITHERS	40	FRANK PARKES	51	GEORGE ATKINS
8	BENJAMIN GRICE	19	ALBERT JONES	30	ISAAC HIPKISS	41	WILLIAM TAYLOR	52	JOSEPH WESTWOOD
9	WILLIAM WESTON	20	WILLIAM HUNTER	31	EBENEZA WOODALL	42	WILLIAM PUGH (CATCH)	53	WILLIAM SIFFORD
10	GEORGE JONES	21	FREDERICK TAYLOR	32	GEORGE MITCHELL	43	MOSES ROSE		
11	JAMES DOWNING	22	JOSEPH DAVIES	33	BERTRAM GUEST	44	J.A. DOBBIE (GENERAL MANAGER)		

Father was intensely patriotic. He never failed to stand rigidly to attention when the National Anthem was being played. If this meant rising during a family meal, as occasionally happened after the advent of the 'wireless', we were all required to emulate his example immediately and without question. At the outbreak of war in 1914, he had voluntarily joined the Royal Army Medical Corps, presumably on the strength of his knowledge and experience of medical matters gained during his membership of the St. John Ambulance Brigade at the Works, where his services were called upon on many occasions. Later, he served with the Royal Engineers. During the latter part of the Great War, he was stationed in Egypt, which he disliked intensely, refusing leave there when the Armistice was signed in 1918, and returning home without delay.

Father in Camp with St. John Ambulance Brigade (Stewarts and Lloyds Division)

Hospital Staff, Haslar Barracks. August, 1914
(Father is back row, extreme right)

Stewarts and Lloyds had promised to keep open the jobs of employees until they returned after the War. However, on his return, Father was very frustrated to find that he resumed his pre-war status, whereas men who had elected to remain at work in preference to active service had been promoted to positions as foremen or as salaried Heads of Departments. He knew that certain of these individuals were far less competent than he – though they were probably far more amiable in temperament – and he never lost his resentment of their promotions.

Aunt Kezia said that Father's temperament was 'spoiled by the War', and that he had become far less patient and more prone to outbursts of uncontrollable temper. These, though short-lived, would upset the family seriously. However, Aunt Maggie (Father's eldest sister) told me that both Father and his father were 'difficult' men – so much so that when her youngest sister, my Aunt Edie, was the only person remaining at home with Grandfather, she decided to emigrate to Australia with a friend. They sailed in December, 1922 on the S.S. 'Esperance Bay'.

Father was keen that we girls should become as independent as possible, and he taught us to do many practical things. His pursuit of perfection pervaded everything he did, and we would hesitate to ask too many questions for fear of getting long, detailed answers starting from basic principles with which we were already familiar.

A consequence of Father's preoccupation with words was his love of poetry – though he had no interest in 'imagination'. He memorised a wide repertoire of poems without difficulty, and occasionally accepted invitations to recite in public. We anticipated these events with anxiety, knowing from experience that he might become so absorbed in the dramatic and emotional content of the poem that he appeared to be on the verge of losing self-control. Restraint was not in his nature, though in fact he was not a demonstrative man.

The daily life of a maintenance engineer in a steel tube factory was by no means easy or congenial. Danger from moving machinery or molten metal was always nearby. Some machines were awkwardly sited and necessitated climbing on to hot steel plates to reach working parts. Often, there would be insufficient time to allow a machine to cool down adequately before inspection, and diagnosis and correction of faults. However, Father saw perfection and beauty in the harmonious integration of the parts of a machine, and therefrom he derived much satisfaction in his work.

Father's temperament was paradoxical in several respects. He could be incredibly patient: yet at times he was singularly impatient, and totally unable to 'tolerate fools gladly'. He was well aware of lacunae in his education: yet he could be arrogant in his display of the knowledge he possessed. He had an acute sense of humour: yet he rarely displayed it, and could certainly never take a joke against himself. He habitually made informed judgements: yet he could be guilty of making a wrong judgement and, in the absence of evidence, of maintaining its validity. He was competent at diagnosing and treating obvious illness and his nursing techniques were sensitive and kindly: yet the existence of illness which was not self-evident could either pass unnoticed or be mis-diagnosed as stupidity or obstinacy. He cared very deeply and conscientiously for his family and was ambitious for our well-being and successful progress through life: yet he failed utterly to appreciate that his ambition and persistence, though capable of giving encouragement, also had the potential to be devastating and destructive.

Mother had a gentler and more equable temperament. When her elder sisters had problems, they came to her for advice; in times of their illness or need, she gave them help and ease. Conversely, when she needed practical help, they gave it willingly. Aunt Kezia was her eldest and most protective sister, and though we sometimes thought her 'bossy', she was the most intelligent and reliable of our aunts.

As a child, Mother attended Halesowen Church School, where the Rector conducted biblical studies in which Mother became well-versed. Needlework, knitting and domestic studies were taught by the Schoolmistress, who, as a special favour to well-behaved children, would send them across to her house to clean and to make rugs for her by 'podging' strips of material into a hessian backing. They also had to scrub and polish the quarried floors and dust and polish her furniture!

My Aunt Kezia, c.1900

The Gorsty Hill children were somewhat despised by the Halesowen children, not only because of their strange speech but also because they arrived at school in dirty boots. They had a long and arduous walk to school, up and down steep inclines on 'dirt' roads.

Before walking to school, Mother sometimes had to collect boxes of boots from her Uncle Simeon Downing's shop in Lodgefield Road and deliver them to local people. For this chore she would sometimes be given a halfpenny. Uncle Simeon made his own deliveries by pony and trap; he was notoriously mean, and Mother's services for next to nothing probably gave him immense satisfaction!

At the age of fourteen, Mother became a student-teacher at Coombs Wood School. Concurrently, she attended classes at Old Hill 'Centre'. She also attended the 'Leasowes', Halesowen, for instruction in dancing, given by the 'Ladies of the Leasowes'. The Leasowes house was originally owned by the poet, William Shenstone, who was more highly regarded for his ability in landscaping and gardening than for his poetry. A few years after his death in 1763, his house was knocked down and replaced by the present house which now serves as a golf clubhouse. During the General Strike of 1926, Father used to take Doris and me to the canal in the grounds of the Leasowes, where he taught us to row in the little boats available for hire at twopence per hour.

The Leasowes, Halesowen
(Permission given by "Birmingham Post & Mail". See acknowledgements)

After their marriage in 1910, my parents appear to have passed a few relatively uneventful years. They did a great deal of walking at weekends, often arriving at the Lickey Hills and Rednal, many miles from home, for Sunday breakfast. They would walk cross-country through fields, passing Hunnington Viaduct which used to carry the rail link between Old Hill Station and the Austin Motor Works at Longbridge. After the line fell into disuse, the Viaduct was demolished; this was our first experience of the loss of landmarks, and a very sad event.

One of the last trains to cross Hunnington Viaduct, travelling from Old Hill Station towards the Austin Motor Works at Longbridge.

(Photographed by W. Hunter, c.1935)

Austin Motor Works, Longbridge, Birmingham, c. 1920

Father was a keen photographer, and he took a picture of one of the last trains to cross the Viaduct. In those days, we found his photography very tedious, because his selection (and sometimes re-arrangement) of subject, setting up of equipment, and calculation of camera settings seemed to take an inordinately long time. Back home again, he would commandeer the cellar and then the kitchen sink for developing and printing. However, his meticulous care resulted in excellent photographs, some of which I still possess in good condition.

When the Great War broke out in 1914 and Father joined the Army, Mother's life became increasingly difficult as food and money became more scarce. Doris was born in 1915 and she had several childhood illnesses including tubercular glands which had to be surgically removed from her neck. This was a fairly common condition in children of those days, as a result of poor nourishment.

Aunt Kezia had been in service in Handsworth, Birmingham, in the house of Dr. Edmund Shaw. She married his son, Dr. Edmund John Shaw on 18th March, 1908. He died on 11th January, 1910, and Auntie Shaw (as she preferred to be called) returned to live in Mafeking Villas. She helped Mother a great deal in nursing Doris and taking her away to convalesce.

Our house was reasonably comfortable but, except for the kitchen, which served as a living room, it was always cold. After my arrival on 6th December, 1919, I had the usual childhood ailments – measles, whooping cough and bronchitis – but nothing life-threatening. Doris and I were given cod liver oil, floating on milk in a spoon, every morning as a preventative against illness. There was a small fireplace in our bedroom, but the room was so small that a fire so near to the bed would have been dangerous. Early on winter mornings, the patterns of frost on the inside of our bedroom windows were fascinatingly pretty; but there was much mopping up of running water when the ice thawed! Feather mattresses, hot water bottles and chilblains remain as vivid memories.

Lighting was by gas lamps in those days, both indoors and out. The lamp-lighter would walk along the streets at dusk with a long pole, on the end of which were a hook and a flint. Stopping at each lamp-post, he would raise his pole through the space in the base of the glass panels of the lamp-shade, and with the hook he would open a valve to allow gas to flow. Simultaneously, the flint would create a spark which ignited the gas in the mantle. At dawn, he would do his round again, extinguishing the light by closing the valve and cutting off the flow of gas. Many of the minor streets had no lighting at all.

Home life revolved around a timetable dictated by Stewarts and Lloyds. The steam-operated hooter, known as the 'bull', signalled the start and finish of work periods, and the walk from work to home and vice versa took twelve minutes. Mother therefore knew exactly the time when a meal had to be on the table, ready for Father's return.

Each day of the week had its routine. The most oppressive was Monday, when the entire day was devoted to washing. Everything was done by hand, very laboriously and thoroughly. There was no running hot water, and the kitchen boiler was heated from underneath by a coal fire. Tuesday was ironing day, and the distinctive smell of freshly-ironed linen (partly deriving from the beeswax with which the plate of the iron was treated to prevent rusting and to keep it smooth) permeated every part of the house.

Whenever we were at home, as in school holidays, we were required to help with the household chores and shopping. We had to darn our own woollen socks and stockings with neat basket-weave darns, leaving a loop at the end of each thread to allow for shrinkage in the wash. Occasionally, on a Saturday afternoon, we were taken to Birmingham, and we even visited the Art Gallery, to see some of the pictures there. At Christmas, we always went to hear a recital of Dickens's *Christmas Carol*, given by a man in the Town Hall. In winter, we sometimes went to Dudley, where we were allowed to buy a hot potato from the man who roasted them in his big black oven in the Market Place. We warmed our hands as we ate them!

Tradespeople would come regularly along our road, with their horses and various shapes of cart, depending on the nature of the goods they offered for sale. They all made their distinctive sounds as they called their wares. There were many additional sounds: the trams, screeching round the corner and round the bend in the tramlines; the trains, as they climbed the gradient in either direction from Old Hill Station; the motorboat, chugging along the canal from the Gorsty Hill tunnel and going on towards Dudley.

Our play times were few and simple. Out of doors, top-and-whip would be in fashion, and would then give way to hoop-and-stick, hopscotch, and a variety of ball games. Indoors, toys were few and were cherished. My favourite was a set of tongued and grooved wooden pieces, with which I could build all kinds of structures; then I could turn some of the pieces on end, calling them children, making desks for them, and playing 'schools' in my little buildings.

Father's holidays were few and unpaid, and therefore rarely taken. Our greatest excitement came when we were taken by train to Portland, where Father had been stationed during the Great War; Mother had visited him there and they had become good friends with a family with whom we went to stay. Father took us to the 'Verne', the huge underground military hospital, and to the quarries, once controlled by Sir Christopher Wren, from which Portland stone had been taken to build St. Paul's Cathedral and many other London churches and famous buildings. We saw St. Peter's Church, built by convicts from the Prison in the nineteenth century, and we were taken all over H.M.S. 'Hood', where Father was in his element, explaining everything in great detail, especially the working of the engines! Portland visits were very impressive and memorable. It is a place of unique interest and great significance.

Postcard received by Mother at the 'Old Cot', postmarked January 2nd, 1904

Portland – The Verne

Chapter 3:

DISPARITY, DESPERATION AND DAMAGE

Before Doris was old enough to go to school, I had made my entry into the world and distracted from her some of the attention to which she had become accustomed. A few months after my arrival she was enrolled at Beeches Road Infant School by the Governess, Miss Wesley. From all accounts, Doris made good but unspectacular progress at school.

My maternal grandmother had been living at our house for some time, and she had frequent attacks of severe bronchitis. I recall my being discovered sitting on her bed, helping to eat her 'Ucal Bronchial Lozenges'. That was deemed to be inappropriate for me at the age of three years! A short time later, on 19th February, 1923, Grandmother died. I remember nothing of the occasion.

Grandmother (Martha Sidaway) with Mother (Sarah Martha Sidaway), c. 1922
Photograph: W. Hunter

After about two years in the Infant School, Doris was transferred to the Junior School where she came under the influence of Mr. Leonard Parkes, a very perceptive and competent Headmaster who was in charge of the school for many years. Whether or not she took the scholarship examination I do not know; but at the age of eleven she passed the Entrance Examination to Wright's Lane Central School, Old Hill, which, many years later, was given Grammar School status.

In the summer of 1926 a cloud descended over the household. Mother contracted scarlet fever, which in those days was a very serious illness. At the time, Father was attending a compulsory training week at a St. John Ambulance Brigade camp, organised by the Firm and held in the grounds of a house at Hartlebury which was the home of one of the Directors. Father was recalled immediately and Doris and I were not allowed to go to school. Auntie Shaw came and made our meals but it was Father who looked after Mother and did all the nursing. We were not allowed to go near to her. A white sheet was pinned over Mother's bedroom door so that no infected flakes of skin could escape to contaminate the air and spread infection.

After about six weeks Mother was able to rejoin us downstairs and there was some semblance of normality. However, Mother seemed always tired and there was an air of gloom and despondency for a long time. The reason for this only became apparent towards the end of the year, at which time there seemed to be no joy at all in the household. Doris was eleven years old and I was seven. On 4th January, 1927, Mary was born. Again, Mother did not leave her bedroom for some time. The doctor came frequently and so did Mrs. Adams, who, though not a qualified midwife, attended most local births and deaths.

Mrs. Adams was heard to say to Auntie Shaw: "Sarah's going to have trouble rearing that one!" Her prognosis was proved correct.

Eventually Mother and 'the baby' rejoined us downstairs. I understand that my comment, made at the time with some pleasure, was: "I'm not the baby, now!" My strongest memory of this time is of the all-pervading smell of 'Milton', which I have always disliked intensely, and of a general sensation of disorder and irritability in the family. However, Doris and I resumed school after the Christmas holiday and a new routine gradually evolved.

Mary was a sickly baby. She had a squint which the doctor advised should not be treated until she was about five years old. When that time came, another doctor blamed Mother for not getting it treated earlier. Meanwhile. Mary had very frequent sore throats and colds, and suffered ill-health more or less continuously. Her tonsils were removed and there was much mopping of her throat with medications.

Mary's first few years coincided with Doris's first years at the Central School. Although Doris's ability to manipulate figures was never her strong point, her English, in all its aspects, was outstandingly good. She submitted an essay in a competition and won first prize – a very large and beautiful copy of *Lorna Doone* which she treasured for many years.

Like Father, Doris was very keenly interested in Shakespeare's plays in general, and in Julius Caesar in particular. She memorised long speeches, which she practised after we had gone to bed at night. As a captive and unwilling audience I developed a very early antipathy towards Shakespeare which I have never really lost. Against my will, I, too, memorised "O mighty Caesar, dost thou lie so low..." without understanding a word of it.

In her last years at Wright's Lane School Doris was a keen member of the Commercial Department. She learned shorthand, typewriting and book-keeping. Her shorthand progress was helped considerably by Father, who would tirelessly dictate timed passages to her in the evenings. Her interest in typewriting was stimulated by the gift of an old typewriter from the Vicar of Rowley Regis, the Reverend F. J. Cheverton, whose Church and Sunday School we attended regularly. She spent many happy hours practising touch-typing and Father taught her how to maintain the machine in good working order and how to effect minor adjustments.

Towards the end of 1930 Mr. Cheverton told us that he was leaving Rowley Regis at the end of the year to become Rector of Byfleet, Surrey. This was quite a blow to my parents. Doris had been attending classes in preparation for Confirmation. At the last minute, I, too, was included, though I had very little idea of the significance of Confirmation. The Service took place just before Mr. Cheverton's departure. His successor was a Yorkshireman who tended to make his sermons political in tone. My parents objected to hearing left-wing politics from the pulpit and our allegiance to Halesowen Church was restored.

At the age of fourteen, Doris left school to take up employment in Old Hill. After a relatively short time, she looked for a more interesting post and obtained one at Netherton. Here, she became friendly with Ivy Chambers who was Captain of 2nd Dudley (St. Francis) Company of Girl Guides. Her enthusiasm was infectious and Doris was enrolled. A short time afterwards, I, too, joined the Company, and before long I became Wren Patrol Leader and Standard Bearer for the Company. As a Church Company we had to attend monthly Church Parades in Dudley. There was no Sunday transport to Dudley so we had to go on our bicycles. Our weekly meetings took place in the Priory Hall, but when the Church of St. Francis was built in the new Priory Estate, Priory Hall was closed and our meetings were held in the Church. A screen was lowered over the Sanctuary so that the Church could be used for many types of activity.

*2nd Dudley (Priory) Girl Guide Company, 1932. Colour Bearers
(Union Jack carried by the author) and the author about to return home
after a Church Parade.*

The Company needed a lecturer in First Aid and Father was invited. He
also helped with knotting, and made a very spectacular display of knots
tied with rope and fixed to a board for the use of the Company. He
was interested in signalling by Morse Code and made sets of electric
buzzers and lights run from torch batteries, for use by the Guides. He
helped with outdoor activities, especially our signalling in Dudley Castle
Grounds over wide distances, and he gave advice on camping, about which
he knew a great deal from his experience with the St. John Ambulance
Brigade.

After a few years, Doris went to work at Stewarts and Lloyds, where she
was soon promoted and became Secretary to the Managing Director, Mr.
Dobbie. During this time, the 'Hollerith' system was introduced to deal
more efficiently with computing of wages and statistics, and Doris was given
responsibility for the use of the main machine, the 'tabulator'.

Working at Stewarts and Lloyds was a 'reserved occupation' during World War II and people were not allowed to leave except to transfer to an alternative 'reserved occupation' or for service in the Forces. At the end of the War, when freedom to move was re-established, Doris left to become Teacher of Typing at Lawrence's College in Birmingham, later to become the Pitman College. She had already obtained a Shorthand Teacher's Diploma and had taught some students at home who were sent to her by the Firm. The teaching of typing appealed to her, and she was appointed as deputy to the Head of Typing, who offered to train her for a Typing Teacher's Diploma, which she gained without difficulty under his expert guidance.

Doris was becoming progressively intolerant of home life, which she did not hesitate to criticise openly, and often very unkindly and unreasonably. She decided to move away, and obtained a post at the Fitzroy College of Commerce in London. There, she became progressively more cynical about her work, feeling that her students were sufficiently affluent to have little incentive to achieve the high standards which she demanded of them. Within a year, she had become totally disillusioned with her work and had decided to leave.

She was appointed to the Royal Normal College for the Blind at Rowton Castle, near Shrewsbury, as Teacher of Typing. She was taught the special skills required in the teaching of typing to blind students by Miss Penny, who gave her a thorough and reliable training. When Miss Penny retired, Doris became Head of the Typing Department, a post which she held until her early retirement on health grounds many years later.

Doris had expert knowledge of her subject and she taught it with meticulous precision and insistence on perfection. She fully understood that her students at Rowton Castle would need their skills in their eventual employment and that they must become totally proficient in order to compete successfully with sighted people. She taught her subject with exemplary efficiency; her students' examination results were proof of this. If her teaching had contained in it an element of humanity and warmth, perhaps she could have been rated an excellent teacher. Her manner, even outside the classroom, was unsympathetic and domineering, though her work was highly regarded by the Principal.

Eventually, Doris began to suffer ill-health. She decided to become non-resident at the Castle and bought a bungalow in the country. Her asthma gradually became worse, until her doctor advised early retirement.

Mary, during her youth, always needed a great deal of attention and supervision. She would be excessively excitable, scribbling vigorously over anything within reach, tearing up paper, throwing toys around and even

At Rowton Castle, near Shrewsbury, 1952
Doris   Mother   Aunt Maggie

Photo: H. Hunter

Doris and Mother near Kerry (Wales), Easter, 1954

Photo: H. Hunter

deliberately damaging any of her toys – or mine – to which she took exception. This kind of behaviour was a new experience in our family. Then Mary would have periods of being anxious and depressed to the point of incessant crying and much wringing of hands, which my parents identified as indicating some kind of physical discomfort.

Doris and I had learned to read and write and to do simple arithmetic long before our schooldays. Mary tended to be rather clumsy in her movements and unco-ordinated – she could never catch a ball in play – and she was very slow to learn anything, either practical or theoretical.

These problems were attributed by my parents to Mary's eye defect. She had an operation to correct her squint at the Children's Hospital in Birmingham. She must have been almost five years old at the time, because there were difficulties about attendance when she started school. She had to be taken back to the hospital, as an out-patient, three times weekly for 'eye exercises', for many months after the operation.

This involved a walk of fifteen minutes to the bus stop, a bus journey of half an hour, usually a long wait before treatment, then the tedious journey home. (I remember this well because at the age of eleven or twelve, I had to take Mary on my own in school holidays, to give Mother some respite.) It was a huge disappointment to Mother when a doctor pointed out, some years later, that Mary's squint had not been corrected. Mother believed it had; but the reverse was all too obvious to all of us.

Naturally, the many days of absence from school interfered with Mary's progress. We all tried to help her to read and write, and no one more so than Father. He could be incredibly patient for a long time – far longer than Mary's span of concentration, which he failed ever to consider. Then his patience would snap and he would become angry at her failure to understand or to make progress. He saw no reason why Mary should not, with perseverance on his part and hers, become just as competent as Doris or myself.

Mary had unfortunate mannerisms which were especially noticeable at mealtimes, which we all came to dread. She would look apprehensively across the table at Father, peering over her spectacles at him. He could not tolerate this and he would become very angry. He would nag her about the way she ate her food, to the point where she 'froze' and became totally incapable of any movement whatever. He saw this as obstinacy and defiance and his fury increased to such a pitch that Mother would take Mary from the table to another room, to protect her until Father had either gone back to work or left the table for some other reason. We would all be upset by this seemingly irrational behaviour of his, which was a frequent occurrence; even when it did not happen, we were anxious lest it should, as Father's outbursts were quite unpredictable.

I sincerely believe that Father intended nothing but good and that he was genuinely incapable of self-control on these occasions. I believe, too, that he had absolutely no idea of the damage he was inflicting, specifically on Mary but in reality on all of us, especially Mother. He really desperately wanted Mary to improve in competence of all kinds. I think it probably never occurred to him that she was physically and mentally limited; if it did, pride would not allow him to admit it.

By the time that Mary was ten years old, the question of her next school had become a matter of some concern to my parents. They consulted Mr. Parkes and were told that examinations were out of the question. This could not possibly have been news to them. The alternative was a school which had a poor reputation. Mr. Parkes put his observations on Mary in a letter which clearly indicates his perceptiveness and tact. It is a totally honest appraisal of her problems. Mary was enrolled as a fee-paying pupil at Stourbridge High School for Girls, which by that time (Autumn 1937) I had recently left. This must have strained the family resources considerably. She seemed to enjoy school but made no progress, and after almost four years there, the Headmistress requested her removal on the grounds that she was occupying a place which should be allocated to a more apt pupil. My parents were upset and offended by this request, but Mary left and stayed at home for a time. She was now fourteen years old.

Letter to Mother from Headmaster of Beeches Road School, Blackheath

After a while, she was enrolled at the Clerks' Training College in Dudley to learn shorthand and typing. This was done at the suggestion of Doris, whose colleague at work had attended there, and recommended it highly. Mary went by bus to Dudley each day and it seemed that she had settled down at last.

One day, I was visiting a school friend of mine in Stourbridge, whose family had come to know ours quite well. In the course of conversation, I was told that Mary was spending a great deal of time at their house.

It transpired that Mary was leaving home ostensibly to go to Dudley, but taking a bus to Stourbridge instead of attending the College. Another family crisis followed. My parents contacted the Principal and asked why no notification of Mary's unexplained and frequent absences had been issued. They were told that she had made no progress in her work, so they asked why they had not been notified of this, either. She was withdrawn from the College forthwith, and stayed at home for a time. Like other mentally unstable people, Mary was not lacking in deviousness.

In 1943 Mary was sent to classes at Halesowen Technical School, to try again to study shorthand and typing. The one interest which she did find there was the Girls' Training Corps which she joined, and became very keen to join the Auxiliary Territorial Service for which the G.T.C. was preparation. As soon as she became eligible at age seventeen, she enlisted. This pleased Father, with his military experience in the Great War.

She went to Guildford for initial training. Some weeks later, my parents were notified that Mary was being discharged from the A.T.S. as being 'temperamentally unsuited' to the Army. She arrived home, bitterly disappointed, exhausted, and utterly depressed. The doctor's advice was sought. He agreed that she would be better working than staying at home permanently, and recommended that, after a reasonable period of rest, Mary should try to get a manual job which was not mentally demanding.

An application was made on Mary's behalf for employment at an electrical components factory on the east side of Blackheath and Mary went to work there. The work naturally enough had advantages and drawbacks. The working day began early and Mary had a long walk (with no available public transport), to reach the factory. She returned home for lunch except when the weather was extremely bad, when she would reluctantly go to the Works Canteen. The working day was long, and on her return home she would be physically very tired. She was somewhat distressed by the smell of oil which permeated her working clothes despite her wearing of a protective overall.

Mary worked at the factory for twelve years, but she was not happy. Sometimes, after she had gone to bed at night, she could be heard whimpering and distressed. She could not communicate any reason for this – she was just utterly miserable and, I believe, exhausted. In those days, just post-World War II, there seemed to be little in the way of appropriate diagnosis or medication for this kind of depression. Whenever possible, I would collect her from work in the car, but this was a fairly infrequent possibility. I took her out into the country as often as I could, and this she always enjoyed.

During one summer whilst I was attending a course in Bridgend, I was recalled home urgently because Mary was ill. When I arrived, she was lying in bed, rigid and unable to speak, unable to take food or drink and obviously desperately needing expert help. My parents hoped that I might somehow enlist the help of an oboe student of mine who was a Neurosurgeon. This I did; he sent a Psychiatric Consultant to our house and Mary was admitted immediately to the Department of Neurosurgery at a Birmingham hospital. She was there for two weeks.

She came home considerably improved. After a lengthy period of convalescence she was deemed fit to return to work. In the years which followed, she had recurrent bouts of mental illness which varied in their manifestation. Sometimes she would be restless but silent, incapable of communication, unable to take food and utterly devoid of energy. At other times, she would wander about the house wringing her hands in her anxiety. She would sometimes be restless and unable to stop talking loudly and continuously through hours of day and night. Nothing would interrupt the flow of her speech on these occasions – an extraordinary situation since normally her conversation was quiet and very limited. This state suggested release from massive repression. The curious thing was that everything she said in these outbursts was related to incidents with which Mother and I were familiar, and the accuracy of detail was astonishing. On other occasions, Mary talked complete nonsense, saying, for instance, that she was dead and that we were all dead, or that everything around her was on fire. When Mary went to her bedroom and began obsessively tidying clothes in her chest of drawers, we knew that an 'attack' of some sort was imminent. Though she seemed unable to control her limbs during these attacks, she never behaved violently towards other people.

The treatment of the day was E.C.T., which Mary had at Birmingham Nerve Hospital as an out-patient; it was very unpleasant and of doubtful efficacy. She was also admitted for varying periods of time to mental hospitals.

At home, we discussed Mary's way of life and decided that she ought to leave the factory. She had by now worked there for twelve years. We suggested to her that my parents would appreciate her help at home as they were getting older. Doris and I agreed to pay her a weekly sum of money so that she would feel she was doing a worthwhile job. This idea appealed to her and the plan was successful over several years. She had relapses, but drugs were being produced which reduced the incidence and severity of her 'attacks'. A régime of treatment by drugs was established and maintained, with only minor changes, throughout the rest of her life. She was by now diagnosed as 'schizophrenic'.

In her better periods, Mary could be meticulous in certain ways. She learned to knit tidily, and, provided that I made up a simple pattern and wrote it out clearly, row by row, she could follow it, ticking off each row as it was completed. I would sometimes return home from my work to find her in an acute state of agitation, just because she had dropped a stitch. When I had retrieved it she would be content again. She made herself a pullover and two dresses, which she wore with pride.

At Lerry Tweed Mill, near Aberystwyth – 1952
Doris, Mary, Mother and me

Photo: W. Hunter

On the Stiperstones in Shropshire, with Mary – 1954
Photo: D. Hunter

For many years, Mary kept a diary. Entries were detailed and tidily written. When we went out in the car, she would make notes which would be transferred to the diary on our return home. If, months later, any of these details needed to be retrieved, Mary would be able to find them and produce them with great satisfaction. (There were blank periods, corresponding with bouts of illness.) The diaries might have been interesting records for reference; unfortunately, Mary was persuaded – much against her will – to allow Doris to destroy them, on the grounds that their content was trivial and no longer relevant. This happened when Mary went to live with Doris in 1973. Persuasion, in Doris's vocabulary, meant insistence, and Mary was given no alternative. This caused Mary unnecessary sadness.

During World War I Father was friendly with a man named Albert Mason. They lost touch after the end of the war, when Father came home immediately but Albert remained to take his leave in Egypt. One day in 1948, Albert appeared unexpectedly at our house, where he was made very welcome. This was the first of many visits.

When he realised that we had no bathroom, Albert organised a conversion which provided one. When he realised that we had no car, he produced one and taught us to drive. Both Doris and I passed our Driving Test at our first attempt but Father was not ready to take the test. This disappointed him; he had expected to learn quickly and then to teach Doris and me. During one lesson, Albert exasperatedly asked Father why he did not move on past traffic lights when they changed to green – then to red and to green again. Father replied that he was working out what was happening in the engine – which valves were opening and which closing, and how the pistons were affected. Albert said that there was no time for such thoughts and that Father should simply think of driving the vehicle and of observing what was going on around him, and there were people waiting behind. Father became impatient, saying that he wanted to understand fully about the car, and people behind would just have to wait! Albert wisely abandoned further attempts to teach Father. After further lessons with professional driving instructors, Father was forced to take their advice and give up the idea of learning to drive. He was temperamentally unsuited to driving; he was the only person who did not realise this.

Albert came from time to time and took us out in his own car, a Jowett Javelin. Mary thoroughly enjoyed these trips because Albert talked to her and was protective. He called on us once when she was ill, and he expressed sympathy with my parents. Father said to him: "Of course, her illness is your fault – you make her too excited!" Albert was deeply hurt, and despite Mother's and my protests that Father's opinion was ridiculous, and untrue, he was most upset, saying that it was hurtful that Father even thought what he said. Albert never came to see us again.

None of us normally had the temerity to argue or to disagree with Father, and life went on. After some months, he said: "I wonder why Albert doesn't come here, now". I said: "Don't you recall insulting him, last time he came?" Father did not, so I reminded him. All he said was: "Well, I was right!" I was furious and told him that he was often right but not in this case, and that he himself had done more to damage Mary's health than anyone else. I cited instances which had remained all too clearly in my memory, such as a time when he was brutally persistent that she should continue to do some arithmetic, when she had, only an hour or so before, had several teeth extracted. (She must have had a great deal of pain from her teeth; by the time she was fifteen, she had full dentures.) I told Father that his excessive ambition for Mary's progress was one of the contributory factors in her mental breakdown, yet he, alone among all of us, had been too blind to appreciate the damage he was doing. My fury subsided; suddenly I felt intensely sorry for him, for he never said a word.

A difficult period followed when Father's health was failing seriously and Mother was stressed beyond reasonable limits. Mary helped as much as she was able, but her health, too, was deteriorating. Doris's infrequent visits were, more often than not, unhelpful. She never missed an opportunity of making derogatory remarks about the house and family, and frequently told Mother how much better Mary's life would have been, had she been less protective and more supportive of Father when he had tried his best to help Mary. This is what Doris sincerely believed. After her departure, it always fell to me to try to put the family together again, as best I could.

We had two wonderful neighbours, Glenis and John Blakeway, who were well aware of the effect of Doris's visits on our household. They were always generous with comfort and sympathy when these were needed, and they gave immense pleasure, especially to Mother and Mary, by their friendship and understanding, and by their quiet and sincere support.

Over the years, the family had become progressively more divided until it was totally and irreparably split down the middle. Mary was in the centre; Father and Doris were on one side and I supported Mother. Mental health problems can tear a family apart; so can pride and excessive ambition.

During 1965, Father had a slight stroke and Mother a mild heart attack within a few days of each other, and Mary reacted badly to the situation. It was Easter time and as I was on holiday I was able to look after them all for a while, at home. When the Summer Term drew near, I had to consider how to deal with the situation. Our Doctor advised me to arrange for Father to go into a Nursing Home, which I did. However, a short time afterwards, he had to be transferred to hospital.

In July, 1967, Father died. Mother's health had improved somewhat, and Mary became a little more stable. Life was relatively peaceful for a few years.

In 1973, Mother fell in the garden and broke her knee-cap. After hospital treatment she made a fair recovery but was unable to walk with confidence again. In August of that year, I had to lecture in Austria, and Doris invited Mother and Mary to stay with her during my absence. Whilst I was away, Mother had a heart attack which was instantly fatal.

Mary remained with Doris, as she could not live on her own at Blackheath whilst I was out at work all day – and some evenings. She continued to live with Doris for some years, during which time she was physically well cared for but very restricted in her activities, partly due to her failing health. She was well-liked by the villagers whom she came to know, and who were sorry for her when they saw how critical and domineering Doris could be with her, even in public. Mary gained sympathy and friendship: Doris lost both.

Continuous medication over many years took its toll on Mary's physical condition and she suffered kidney failure. Following a fall and a fractured femur, she developed pneumonia and died in hospital at Ludlow on 23rd July, 1997, at the age of seventy.

Mary had always been known to our neighbours and friends in Blackheath as a warm, friendly person, always ready to give help to others, within the limits of her capacity to do so. She had no pride, and she was incapable of being offensive in any way. Our friends always showed her great kindness and understanding and she enjoyed their company. She is remembered with affection by those people who knew her well, and at the same time, with sadness that her life had not been a happier one. Perhaps she may now have found the peace which eluded her throughout her lifetime.

Chapter 4:

FOUNDATIONS, FRIENDS AND FREEDOM

The tray on my heavy dark wooden high chair had a semi-circular wire on which were threaded ten rather large coloured balls. I well remember counting them, dividing them into groups, adding and subtracting, and multiplying in twos. I am sure I did not know the correct terminology for what I was doing. Working out a two times table (within the limits of ten balls) was knowledge acquired with pleasure and a sense of achievement at a very early age. Concurrently, since my porridge arrived on a dish with the alphabet decorating its perimeter, I learned to manipulate letters in my mind, spelling the shorter words with which I was already familiar in speech, and learning to recite the alphabet forwards and also backwards.

The exact duration of the high chair era, and the amount of help and encouragement I had during that time, I do not recollect. The fact remains that, when I first went to school, in 1925 aged five, I could read and do simple arithmetic without difficulty.

I was eager to go to school. For a long time I had heard the bell, in the little tower above Powke Lane Board School, Blackheath, ringing from 8.55 to 9.00 a.m. every school day, and I was delighted when my turn came to respond to it.

Mother took me to school on my first morning, but after that I always went and returned on my own, despite my having to dodge the trams as they screeched round the corner into Perry Park Road.

The Governess of the Infant School was Miss Downing, a very portly lady who always wore a long black dress, covered by a black apron tied round her waist. She had her own class of about fifty children in a dull, darkly-painted room, and no child was allowed to speak unless spoken to. Our desks, with seats attached, were heavy wooden affairs, held together on iron frames. Each desk seated two children and we sat in rows facing the blackboard, with arms folded behind and 'heads up straight' in the approved manner of those days. We sometimes did physical exercises in the classroom. These involved stepping into the aisles between rows of desks and doing arm stretching and bending exercises, marking time, or running on the spot with knees raised as high as possible, consistent with avoiding bruising on the edges of the desks. We did deep breathing exercises, but the air quality in that dusty dark room must have been very questionable!

I was soon promoted to Miss Edwards's class. She was a younger teacher than Miss Downing, not blessed with good looks, and with prominent teeth; but in my five-year-old opinion, she had the most wonderful singing voice. She taught us many songs and hymns and I enjoyed everything about life in her class – except the squeaking of slate pencils as we wrote on our slates.

During the summer holiday my parents took Doris and me to Portland. One day we all went on a sea trip from Weymouth to nearby Lulworth Cove. The sea was very rough and as the boat was tossed about, I sat contentedly on a coil of rope on the deck, singing the songs and hymns which Miss Edwards had taught us. I stopped singing and immediately a lady nearby, who had been listening, said: "Oh, don't stop singing or I shall be sick!" Embryonic 'music therapy', perhaps?

At Portland with Mother – c.1925

Photo: W. Hunter

At Portland

Photo: W. Hunter

I recall an occasion when a composition I had written merited my taking it round the school and reading it aloud to each class in turn. We were 'Mixed Infants' and the boys had written about 'Girls' and the girls about 'Boys'. I wrote that I did not like boys. My exact words were: "They scratch, kick, pinch and fight. The only boy I like is Eddie Wheeler". There was no problem until I came to Eddie's class. There he was, golden-haired and freckled, in a tidy brown pullover – a real charmer. I don't remember which of us was the more embarrassed! I never saw him again after the tender age of six!

After having been 'Mixed Infants' for an appropriate period of time we were promoted to the 'Big School' and segregated. We all entered through the same outer door, then the boys turned left into Mr. Johnson's school and the girls turned right into Miss Woodall's school. She was a large and formidable lady who always wore a long brown silk dress. She rarely moved from her desk and frequently leant forward, peering over her spectacles as if challenging any child to move or to raise her eyes from work in hand. When she did speak, her voice was low-pitched and sinister, and she commanded respect without effort. Her desk was in the classroom – as were all headteachers' desks in those days – and she had a clear view of three classes, each of about fifty children, separated only by movable partitions of wood and glass, which were sometimes folded back along floor runners to make one large class for such activities as hymn-singing practice.

Sometimes, the 'Nits' lady would come in to speak to Miss Woodall, then she would come and inspect all our heads. We had to put faces down on our desks whilst she raked through our hair with bony fingers. She was tall and gaunt, and she always wore the same grey tailored pin-striped suit which exaggerated her awesome appearance.

I remember very few specific lessons of that period of my life, though some do remain clearly in my mind. I recall needlework lessons in one class. We each had to make for ourselves a pinafore in blue cotton material. Both back and front were full length, joined by seams at the shoulders and by a tab at the waist on each side. The feature which made these pinafores so memorable was the bias binding. We had to cut 'crossway strips' from a triangular piece of white material (very difficult without stretching it diagonally) and stitch them together at the correct angle to make a continuous length of binding, which we had to tack and then stitch very carefully and tidily all the way round both back and front of the pinafore. Then we had to turn the binding over the raw edge of the blue material, turn it in, then tack and hem all the way round. It is no wonder that this activity stayed clearly in my mind until now, for the whole procedure must have occupied many weeks of needlework lessons!

We also had knitting lessons in which we had to make a pair of bedsocks. I knitted mine in white wool on steel needles and after each lesson all our knitting was put away in a cupboard until the following week. Each time my white knitting re-appeared, it had developed a new brown streak across it. The unhappy alliance of steel needles and perspiration from my fingers produced permanent rust stains which marked weekly increments in my work!

The boredom of needlework and knitting assignments was second only to that of painting and drawing lessons. An eight-year-old is not immediately inspired by the appearance of a blue stone jam jar, set up on a desk; to have to draw and paint it is exceedingly tedious.

One day, boredom was alleviated by the arrival of two piles of shiny new books. The brown ones were all called 'In the Days of the Pharaohs' and the blue pile were 'Norse Legends'. We were allowed to take a book each and to read silently at specific times during each day, which was a great treat. Life in school was indeed very quiet in those days; speaking in class was a sin and conversation was only permitted at playtime.

The 'Top Class' of the school was presided over by Miss Prudence Bennett, another very heavily-built lady who moved little and talked a lot. Sometimes we had to process in single file through another classroom (ruled by a teacher whom we feared greatly because she bounced around and shouted) into Miss Bennett's classroom. There, we had to stand silently and listen to performances by her two favourite pupils, Maggie and Margaret, as they recited prayers and passages from the Bible, most of which we didn't understand. We listened to: "Prevent us, O Lord, in all our doings...", "And I saw a new Heaven and a new Earth...", and we were exhorted to "Consider the lilies of the field..." These passages were delivered in unison by Maggie and Margaret in frightfully exaggerated high-pitched singsong voices; they went up together and came down together and we marvelled at their expertise. Then we trailed silently back to our classroom, presumably morally and aesthetically enriched by the experience.

The worst feature of our school was the toilet block. Its position in the furthest corner of the playground demonstrated the admirable sensitivity of nineteenth century architects. The toilets were damp and dark, with half-doors like stable doors; the smell also was reminiscent of stables, familiar in those days of horse-drawn transport. Construction was simple and basic: a wide crock pipe, leading down vertically into the bowels of the earth. Mother must have known about these places, because she always told me not to use them and to wait until I returned home. I remember being in some discomfort, at the end of one morning, as we made our customary appeal to the Lord to be present at our table and reminded Him that we hoped to feast with Him in Paradise sometime later. I personally had a far more pressing problem, which I failed to solve satisfactorily, and I had a somewhat damp five minutes' journey home.

One day, when I was playing across Highfields, I ran down a bank and my head travelled faster than my feet would go. I fell on my arm and hurt it badly. When I arrived home it was put in a sling and I was taken to Dudley Guest Hospital. The journey was by tram; the seats were made of wooden slats and there was a great deal of painful jolting. There was a long walk from the tram terminus to the hospital, and even now I can remember feeling desperately weary by the time that Mother and I arrived there. My arm proved to be broken – a 'greenstick fracture of the humerus' they said.

My arm was fastened with sticking plaster to a splint made of two pieces of wood fixed together at right-angles, then it was bandaged and supported by a sling. After several weeks, the splint was removed and my arm had set rigidly with the forearm at right-angles to the upper arm. This had to be remedied by physiotherapy at the hospital. The procedure was fairly crude in the 1920's. I was required to pick up and put down repeatedly a zinc bucket half-filled with sand. I didn't enjoy that but I practised at home between visits to hospital and eventually my arm resumed its intended shape.

During my 'sling' period, I was chosen to make a presentation to a lady who opened the Church Garden Party. Her gift was a very large rose-bowl which I had to carry up on to a platform. I was so concerned to get myself and the rose-bowl safely up the steps that I forgot completely what I was supposed to say, but I don't think that mattered, in the circumstances!

A short time before I left Powke Lane Board School, it was elevated to the status of 'Blackheath Junior Mixed School', despite the fact that we were totally segregated. We were encouraged to buy and to wear navy-blue cadet-style caps, trimmed in green with the monogram B.J.M.S. They must have looked fairly ridiculous, but we were proud of them as one small step towards real school uniform!

It was about that time that I learned to ride our family bicycle, a large, heavy pre-First-World-War machine with twentyeight-inch wheels. Doris, with her longer legs, could sit on the saddle and ride it properly, and we used to go out together delivering Church magazines. I had to sit on the carrier, made of metal bars spaced apart, behind the saddle. One day, she rode into a pot-hole which jolted the bicycle so hard that the carrier stays slipped on the fork of the back wheel and I was sorely pinched between carrier bars and rear mudguard.

On another occasion, Doris asked me if I would like to try to ride. I welcomed the idea, handed over the remaining magazines to her, and mounted the pedals of the bicycle. I could not reach the saddle. After some wobbling, I began to feel more secure and I rode away and out of sight. I cannot remember how long my first journey was, but eventually I returned home to find a very sullen Doris, still clutching Church magazines. After that, we were for ever competing for the use of the bicycle. Mother told me, years later, that well-meaning neighbours often told her that I should get killed, riding around on the pedals, but I didn't.

In 1929, my two aunts, Eliza Reavley and Isabella Brown (Father's two older sisters), came south from North Seaton to stay with Aunt Maggie in Harborne, Birmingham. At the end of their holiday. they took me back with them to spend a holiday at Aunt Eliza's home.

North Seaton was a mining village in Northumberland, just north of the River Wansbeck, which could be crossed by Cambois Ferry. The Colliery workings, I was told, extended for a mile or so, out under the sea. The little houses had been built in uniform rows of identical houses by the Colliery owners, for their employees. Each house had one living room and a kitchen, and two bedrooms upstairs.

Toilets were outside across a small yard. They faced the house and backed on to a dirt road. Their design was simple: a wooden bench seat with two holes – one adult size and one child size – and a supply of newspaper. A small door opened into the back road, allowing the 'nightman' to run his truck along the steel rails laid for the purpose, and to collect the contents from the toilet of each house.

When Uncle Will Reavley was due to return from his work in the Colliery (where he was also a 'Union' man, much to Father's displeasure), I had to disappear and visit Aunt Isabella at No. 4, Third Single Row, a few minutes' walk away. She was a widow, my uncle David having been killed in a pit accident a few years previously. She was left to bring up my four cousins on a pittance. The eldest went to work in the colliery and he, too, was killed in an accident. The next cousin, a daughter, used to clean for my Aunt Eliza, in order to earn a little money for the family. She resented the attitude of Aunt Eliza's daughter (her cousin), who was a teacher in the area.

Towards the end of each afternoon, Aunt Eliza heated water over the coal fire and prepared a hot bath, ready for the return of Uncle Will from the pit. The bath was placed in front of the living room fire, and when Uncle Will came home, black and grimy and smothered in pit dust, he took over the living room, undressed, bathed, and transformed himself into a tidy 'gentleman'. He was a local councillor and well respected. Aunt cleared away after him, and living room life resumed normality.

After my holiday I was put on the train at Newcastle on Tyne and my parents met me at Birmingham.

The pits inevitably closed, and when I last visited Northumberland, all the pit-head structures – winding gear and buildings - had gone, as had the rows of little Colliery houses.

Postcard sent by Aunt Isabella to Father at 6 Coombs Wood Building, postmarked 8th April, 1905, and showing the 'Rows' of miners' houses (front view), in North Seaton, Northumberland, demolished many years ago.

About 1929 there was a general sorting-out of Mixed Juniors according to their addresses and I was transferred to Beeches Road Junior Mixed School. I was there for about a year, during which time I was shunted from class to class every few weeks. Before long, I found myself in the top class of about fifty pupils, taught by another Miss Downing who was very pleasant and encouraging. In this school each class consisted of both boys and girls, but they sat in separate groups. Each day began with prayers, then the register was called. On a Monday, War Savings (later called National Savings) were collected and stamps issued. Modulator Practice took place most mornings, and I learned to sing scales and to make my voice leap up and down according to the tonic solfa syllables indicated with a pointer by Miss Downing. We learned to sing sharpened and flattened notes, by means of which we could, with some excitement, move into another key and out again.

I had been having piano lessons for a short time, but I disliked my piano teacher and I knew that the dislike was mutual. She was thin and grey and spoke in a squeaky voice, and she criticised me for arriving for my lessons without a hat. I remember an occasion when she put a piece of music on the piano in front of me and said : "Read that!" So I read "C, B, G, C..." She said: "No, I mean play it!" I said: "I thought you said read it." She said that was the same thing, but I could not understand her reasoning. In my somewhat precocious mind, this was typical of adult misuse of words, and was on a par with being told: "Put up your left hand – yes, that's right!" She would say: "Play staccato, staccato..." and I didn't understand that, either. She demonstrated her meaning by jabbing a note from above and lifting her whole arm high above the keys. I was expected to imitate her movements, but when I did so, I jabbed the wrong key and my fingers landed anywhere but in the right places afterwards. I hadn't the faintest idea what was the purpose of this performance anyway, and she never told me. Sometimes she would say that my rhythm was wrong, without explaining what rhythm meant. I think she gave me up as a total failure in music. For my part, I was always delighted when her companion answered the door and said that I couldn't have a lesson because Miss S. was ill!

I used to whistle a great deal, much to the annoyance of the family, who tried to stop me by saying that I would grow up with ugly lips. One day at school, I was running away from a boy (as I frequently did) and I fell in the playground, opening up a great gash in my chin. Miss Downing took me home, since there was no doctor at the local surgery, and Father was sent for from the Works. He somehow stopped the bleeding and dressed the wound, fixing the dressing with a four-tailed bandage. A long piece of broad bandage was slit at both ends leaving the centre intact to cover my chin dressing. The two lower ends were taken up beside my face and tied on top of my head, and the two upper ends were taken round my neck and tied, then the four ends were united behind my head. The doctor came, later in the day, and decided against stitching but recommended that the same style of bandaging be continued. Whistling inside a four-tailed bandage is virtually impossible and peace fell upon the family. However, they were so relieved when my chin healed and no longer needed dressings and I returned to good health – and to my old habit of whistling – that they never again tried to stop me!

I was asked to play the piano at school so that the children could march in step with each other from the playground into their class-rooms. I played the same monotonous march twice a day, until eventually Mr. Parkes, the Headmaster, asked: "Don't you know another one?"

I spent the latter part of my time at Beeches Road in Mr. Parkes's specially selected 'Scholarship Class'. We worked hard, mainly on our own in Miss Downing's room. Whenever he was free to do so, Mr. Parkes taught us personally. We worked through past Scholarship Papers set by a variety of

Education Authorities in England and Wales and collected in a book with a purple cover. We did homework – strictly without parental help, so that our weaknesses could be identified – and I loved it! Ultimately, several of us sat the Scholarship Examination at a school in Old Hill. This was on a wintry day in March, 1930. We had to walk the mile or so through deep snow to Old Hill, and back again at the end of the day.

During the summer of that year, we went on a day trip from school to New Brighton. On our arrival back at Old Hill Station about midnight that night, I was met by my anxious parents who insisted on speaking to Mr. Parkes. I did not know what this was all about, but it transpired that they had received a letter, after my departure that morning, bidding me to attend, on that very day, an interview in connection with the award of a scholarship. Mr. Parkes, as was his wont, sorted out the problem, and the interview took place later. I was eventually awarded a Staffordshire 'Minor D' Scholarship and the school was given a day's holiday to celebrate my success. I think my parents were pleased, too, but they never showed their pleasure particularly, nor gave any reward, since success was expected as a matter of course. When other children had gifts to celebrate success my parents were disdainful, taking the view that being given a reward was demeaning!

On my application form to sit the scholarship examination, I had been asked to state my first and second choices in the event of success. My first choice had been Halesowen Grammar School and my second Oldbury Grammar School. So Staffordshire Education Committee, in its wisdom (for which I have always been grateful) gave me a free place at a Worcestershire school – the County High School for Girls, Stourbridge – which had moved from premises in the local Library to beautiful new buildings at the top of the hill out of the town only two years previously.

I started school at Stourbridge in September, 1930, at the age of ten years. I had to walk from home in Blackheath to Old Hill Station to catch the 8.34 a.m. train to Stourbridge Junction. On the train were several senior girls who took me with them to school. At Stourbridge Junction we had to go through an underpass to another platform to catch the 'Motor Train' to Stourbridge Town Station, and from there we walked up to School.

This was the beginning of independence and opportunity for me – a totally different way of life in a new environment. I returned home each evening, but my lifestyle at Stourbridge was outside the experience of my parents, who wisely left me to deal with it very much on my own.

There were still the demands of home life to be met, such as helping with the washing-up and responding to Mother's frequent exasperated remark: "Can't you put that book down and do something useful!" On the whole, however, I was allowed to get on with my homework – albeit in a cold room –

and to satisfy the demands of school. In the holidays there were my expeditions to Birmingham Children's Hospital to take Mary for eye treatment, and a certain amount of general attention to her needs at home. When I wanted to go out with school friends, Mother would frequently say: "Take Mary with you – she will enjoy that", and then I would not go myself because I knew that it would be inappropriate to take Mary and unkind not to do so. We had few visitors at home because they were not encouraged; I could never ask school friends back home because Mother felt she would be embarrassed when they saw our little house. I think she was wrong, but the fact remained that home and school were kept quite separate.

The Headmistress of my new school was Miss Ethel M. Firth who had taught Mother many years before. She was dignified, very prim, and meticulous in every way. Staff and girls respected her and the school was a model of good behaviour, immaculate appearance and academic achievement; at the same time, it was a very happy school. On her retirement in 1933, Miss Firth was succeeded by Miss B. M. Dale, who maintained the high standards already established.

The new girls had to take a reading test with Miss D. P. Eastwood, who taught various subjects to the lower forms and singing throughout the school. The reading test took place just inside the Assembly Hall, and we went in to Miss Eastwood one by one. In my test I came to the word 'daïs' which was new to me. I pronounced it as "daze" then asked what it meant. Miss Eastwood explained the effect of the diaeresis and indicated the raised platform at the end of the Assembly Hall, as an example of what the word meant. She was so patient and kindly that I felt totally at ease in conversation with her. She was to influence my life greatly in later years.

The girls who had scholarships were placed in Form 2 Upper, and our Form Mistress, Miss C. J. Voyce, was also new to the school. She specialised in history and also taught junior Latin, so she taught us often. She was one of the best teachers in the school, not only because of her thorough knowledge of her subjects but also because of her infectious enthusiasm for them and for our general all-round development of interests, both academic and sporting. I was not only in her Form but also in her House – Violet House – and throughout my school life Miss Voyce was a great support and a good friend.

During my second term at school, I fell whilst playing leapfrog over a sixth-form girl along a concrete corridor, one wet lunchtime. Again, I broke my left arm and I was said to have 'fractured the two epicondyles of the left humerus' which sounded very grand but was excruciatingly painful – more especially so since pain-killers were not offered in those days with the gay abandon of today. This time, my arm was attached to a straight splint from

Staff of County High School for Girls, Stourbridge, c.1932
Back: *Miss Gibson, Miss Wells, Miss Davis, Miss Voyce, Miss Fanthorpe and Miss McDonald*
Front: *Miss Sneyd, Miss Eastwood, Miss Dromgoole, Miss Cooke, Miss Firth (Head Mistress),*
Miss Tilley, Miss Edwards, Miss Chance and Miss Emms

shoulder to hand, and after six weeks of immobility I was hard-pressed to get it to bend again at the elbow. The recommended 'physiotherapy' was to place my hand against a wall and walk towards it! Somewhat miraculously, full mobility was eventually restored.

I think that I never really recovered from that long absence from school at such a critical point in my education. I kept up reasonably well with my form-mates but not as well as I would have liked. Fortunately, classes were quite small – usually about twentyfive girls in a class and rarely as many as thirty – so we each had a fair share of attention.

I enjoyed not only the lessons but also all the physical activities in school. We had at least one gymnastics lesson each week and also hockey and netball in winter and tennis and cricket in summer, so that there was some sport every day. In addition, there was almost an hour between the end of school dinner and the beginning of afternoon lessons, and whenever the weather allowed, we organised our own team games in the field or on the tennis courts. We also had inter-house competitions and our school teams played matches against neighbouring schools. One of our favourite opponents was Cadbury's Netball Team; when we played them at Bournville we were always allowed to swim, afterwards, in their wonderful large swimming pool.

We had good food in those days. I always had to eat a cooked breakfast before leaving home and this consisted of bread fried in beef dripping with fried egg or fried tomatoes or cheese. No one ever mentioned 'calories'! Then at mid-morning break we had one-third of a pint of full-cream milk every day, with, sometimes, a wholemeal biscuit. School dinners were very adequate, costing eightpence a day, and they always concluded with a substantial 'pudding'. Home for tea, which was bread-and-butter and home-made jam and cake; before bedtime there would be a more than adequate supper. So it was just as well that we played plenty of sport. I have always lived with a weight problem but I've never lacked strength and stamina!

My friends and I used to cycle a great deal, too. I bought a bicycle from one friend for seven shillings and sixpence (well under fifty pence in present-day money). It had no bell or light and very little in the way of brakes, but I remedied those defects and painted it, and it lasted for many years and carried me many miles.

I had no outstanding strengths, either in academic work or in sports, but I had no particular weaknesses, either. I was selected for school sports teams and I joined every school society for which I was eligible. I belonged to the Art Club, the Musical Society, the Historical Society and when I reached the fifth form the Scientific and Geographical Society also.

Society meetings took place after school and they were preceded by school tea, available at a cost of fourpence, for which we were given tea, bread and butter with jam, and cake made in the school kitchen. After meetings, I had to catch a later train home, and if I had to wait some time on Stourbridge Junction Station, I could go into the Ladies' Waiting Room where there was always a good coal fire, and I could do some of my homework.

In the fourth form we were allowed to apply for auditions to join the School Choir. Needless to say, I did so, and after my singing 'The King of Love my shepherd is' and taking breath only at approved places, Miss Eastwood accepted me. During that year, we had an Open Evening at school, and Father attended. He told me, after we had returned home, that Miss Eastwood had spoken to him during the evening. I asked what had been said, and he told me that she had said that his daughter was quite a promising musician. He had replied that she must be mistaken – he was Hilda Hunter's father!

We attended weekly choir rehearsals, learned descants for our hymns, and practised the correct pointing of the psalms which we sang every Friday. We gave occasional performances in school and on special occasions such as Speech Day, and at Christmas we visited the local Workhouse to sing carols to the inmates.

The only music taught in school was singing which took place once a week for forty minutes, with several classes together. Miss Eastwood was a delightful teacher whom I admired greatly. She had great poise and dignity, and she was always as gracious as she had been on my first day at school. Her speaking and her singing voice were the most exquisite sounds I had ever heard.

I remember feeling depressed one day, as I was returning home from school. I was doing moderately well in all subjects, and enjoying them greatly; but I did so wish that I could be really good at something – anything. Some of the girls in my form were exceptionally good at one subject or another. One of my friends was brilliant at French and another at geography; another would get ninety-plus percent in every examination, and wonder where the odd marks had been lost! This was all very demoralising. However, I plodded on and tried to keep up with them all.

Badge of Stourbridge Girls' High School, Worcestershire depicting the fruit-growing industry, the Malvern Hills and the River Severn.

Form V lower A with Miss Voyce
1933-1934
(The author is second from right, front row)

Chapter 5:

PIPES, PROBLEMS AND PROGNOSES

I was fourteen when my life took on a whole new dimension at a cost of fivepence-halfpenny.

After one school holiday, tall bamboo poles appeared in a shadowy corner of the vestibule outside the Music Room. Miss Eastwood told us that she had been on a course during the holiday and had learned to make a bamboo pipe; she offered to share this new skill with any girls who were interested.

Of course I was interested, and so were several other girls, so we went along at the appointed time. Miss Eastwood showed us her pipe and played a tune on it. Then she distributed copies of instructions and showed us the basic tools which we would need to use. She handed to each of us a length of bamboo, suitable for making a so-called 'treble' pipe and a cork for making the mouthpiece. The cost was fivepence for the pipe and a halfpenny for the cork making a total cost, in present-day terms, of just under two pence.

We used an auger to bore out the membrane from within the joint of the bamboo and we made two saw-cuts at an angle to each other to make a mouthpiece. We made a hole with a sharp edge on its further side so that a sound would be produced when air was blown towards it. That hole was called the 'window' and we had to make a channel leading to it from the mouthpiece. The airway and mouthpiece were completed by shaping and inserting the cork, and at this stage a note could be produced. The note was lower than the desired pitch and we had to saw short lengths from the lower end of the bamboo until the correct pitch for the lowest required note, D, was obtained. The positions of holes to be bored along the tube were then marked, and the holes were made, one by one beginning with the lowest, with a reamer. The fingering system was to cover all holes for the lowest note, then to raise them one by one to produce successive notes of the major scale. Two additional notes were obtained by 'cross-fingering' – the process of closing some holes lower down the tube than some open ones. One or two girls fell by the wayside, but a small number of us completed our pipes – though with varying degrees of success in terms of the quality of the sound they were capable of producing. The whole process was to me tremendously satisfying and I enjoyed a wonderful sense of achievement.

Father took a great interest in my pipe-making and from time to time suggested improvements in technique. He introduced me to more appropriate tools which facilitated greater accuracy. He fixed a small vice to the table in the toolhouse and lined its jaws with wood so that they would hold the slippery bamboo more firmly and would be less likely to damage it. He suggested fashioning the mouthpiece with a very sharp knife, in preference to making saw-cuts which might split the bamboo. Though neither he nor I knew it at the time, this resulted in my making a mouthpiece of the same shape as that of the conventional recorder. (Recorders were at that time only just emerging from many years of oblivion and were not the ubiquitous instruments which they are today.) Father also bought me a hand drill and a set of drill bits, again with a view to avoiding the splitting of the bamboo and in order to produce a good shape of hole. An additional refinement was made possible by the use of a countersink bit by means of which I could take the edge off each hole, ensuring comfortable and safe finger holds.

I made many pipes, some for girls who were not interested in making them but wanted to play them, and some for members of Staff and even for the new Headmistress. I still have my own very first pipe, made in 1934 and now celebrating its sixty-fifth year! I subsequently made others which looked better, but their sound was not quite so good. My original one is now somewhat battle-scarred, but I play it, and it still has a lovely gentle sound.

We made pipes of varying bore and length, and therefore of different pitch levels, and we played quartets and trios under Miss Eastwood's guidance.

When Speech Day was in prospect, Miss Eastwood asked me if I would play a pipe solo. She allowed me into the hallowed area of the music cupboard, which was, in fact, a small room lined with shelves from floor to ceiling and containing a great deal of music for voices. She suggested that I look through the music and find something which I would like to play. Since the bamboo pipe is restricted in range, I had to use a trial-and-error technique of transposing songs into a key which made them playable on the pipe. This was invaluable experience – far more useful than learning what transposition is and then doing exercises!

My 'pipe solo for Speech Day' became an annual institution, and among the pieces I played were 'Where e'er you walk' (Handel), 'Art thou troubled' (Handel) and 'I attempt from love's sickness to fly' (Purcell). I had to invent fingerings for some of the accidentals and that, too, was good experience.

We had one very kindly member of Staff who taught scripture, among other subjects. She knew about my interest in music, and asked me one day if I had heard a certain performance on the 'wireless' the previous evening. I said: "No, Miss Cooke, we haven't got a wireless." She replied: "Oh, you poor dear!" and the lesson continued. I relayed this conversation in its entirety to my parents that evening. They were too proud to tolerate pity, and a very few days later, a brand new 'Murphy wireless' was bought and installed in our house!

Time went on and in the summer of 1935, School Certificate examinations came round. I got a reasonable result though not a brilliant one. I passed in all my subjects with some credits, but I did not achieve matriculation standard overall.

One day in the autumn term of 1935, Miss Eastwood was talking to me about pipe playing and she said that I ought to try playing a clarinet or an oboe. I said that I did not know what a clarinet or an oboe were, and she told me that they were orchestral wind instruments. There, the conversation ended. I went home and told my parents and there was little reaction. However, after some days had passed, Father came home with a parcel. This proved to be an oboe, the property of the Firm, which had once had an orchestra for which it provided some of the instruments. The orchestra had disbanded some time previously and the instruments were in store. Father had been allowed to borrow the oboe for a few weeks.

I had not the faintest idea what to do with it because I had never seen a reed before, and all my attempts to get a sound were failures. However, the next day was a Saturday and I was to play in an 'away' netball match. On the coach I happened to sit next to the gymnastics mistress, Miss McDonald. She talked to me about my music and I told her about the arrival of the oboe at home, and how I could not make a sound on it. She said: "Well, my landlord plays an oboe – he is the only person in Stourbridge who does – and if you like, I will arrange for you to meet him and he may be able to help you!"

I duly went to see Mr. Glover – a blacksmith by trade – and he gave me a good reed and showed me how to get a sound. He lent me an oboe tutor and I went home in the best of high spirits. Practising was physically very exhausting because the reed I had was very hard, and I had to make an enormous effort with breath and lip pressure to produce reasonable sounds. However, I had a series of lessons from Mr. Glover during October and November, 1935.

One day, Mr. Glover asked me if I would like to play second oboe to him in the Stourbridge Concert Society Orchestra. He had already discussed the possibility with the conductor, Mr. Frank Edwards, who happened to have two daughters at the High School and who had therefore heard my Speech Day pipe solos. Mr. Glover took me to my first orchestral rehearsal where I was warmly welcomed by Mr. Edwards. I played in my first orchestral concert – a performance of Handel's *Samson* – in December, 1935. I am sure that my tone quality could not have been described as 'refined', but I was very much encouraged by members of the orchestra and by Mr. Edwards, who, in later years, was to become a very good friend and a great source of wisdom.

A short time later, the Firm asked for the return of their oboe and Father took it back. This was a great blow to me, and, armed with five pounds, I scoured Birmingham and made enquiries at the various music shops about oboes for sale, but there were none. So I found Yardley's in Snow Hill, about which Mr. Glover had told me. It was a jewellers-cum-pawn shop. They had an oboe which I bought for four guineas. I took it to Mr. Glover, who said that it was a 'high pitch' instrument, but as I had managed to solve that problem with the Firm's oboe, I would probably manage to do so again. I played that little oboe quite happily for some time and in several more concerts.

Miss Eastwood now said that I ought to consider the possibility of my having oboe lessons from a professional oboe teacher, and that she had begun making some enquiries. She had discovered that Miss Lucy Vincent taught oboe at the Birmingham and Midland Institute School of Music, but that she would be willing to give me some private lessons at her home in Edgbaston. I went to see her and had my first lesson.

Miss Vincent immediately put me at my ease and I liked her very much. She was very positive and direct in her manner and in her advice and criticism. She listened to my playing and her first advice was that my progress to date merited my having a good professional instrument, without which I would be severely limited. She explained about standards of pitch and said that I must have an instrument of 'concert pitch' in order to play with established orchestras; my present little oboe was 'high-pitch' and though I could manoevre it into tune, that was no longer good enough. She told me about makes and prices and I went home armed with information. My parents listened to my news and were wise enough, in matters of which they had no experience, to take the advice of a specialist.

Lucy (as I was now permitted to call her) ordered a new Louis oboe for me at a cost of £52; but she gave me the benefit of her professional discount and it cost me £39. Even that was a considerable outlay of money in 1936, but it proved to have been money well spent. I have the oboe now, in as good condition as when it was new.

Lucy was a very experienced player; she was Principal Oboe in the City of Birmingham Orchestra and in the BBC Midland Orchestra and she did professional playing around the Midlands. She was an excellent teacher, encouraging but also meticulously critical, and no flaw escaped her sensitive ear. Nothing less than excellence would satisfy her, yet she never failed to be kindly and encouraging. I was introduced to more comfortable and more easily controlled reeds and my playing was rebuilt to her demanding standards.

Lucy Vincent

Lucy's own playing was much admired by the conductors for whom she played, principally Sir Adrian Boult and his pupil and successor as conductor of the CBO in 1930, Leslie Heward. She knew countless famous professional conductors and players of her day, and was revered by all those who knew her well. She took me to a recital by her friend, Leon Goossens, and introduced me to him, which was a great honour for me. I was privileged in having her as my teacher and we remained good friends for the remainder of her life. I enjoyed working very hard to satisfy her high standards and to make them my own. My performance improved spectacularly and I became involved in more and more playing.

Meanwhile, after the end of my lower sixth year at school in July, 1936, there began a brief period of uncertainty. I still had no plans for my future, and the question arose as to whether I should return to school after the summer holiday. The headmistress had written in my report that she hoped I would return for another year. However, Doris, who was now well established at Stewarts and Lloyds, had other ideas. She arranged for me to go for an interview in the hope that I would be employed by the Firm. I resented this interference but I attended the interview.

Doris was furious when she saw me arrive in my school dress and blazer, and my panama hat trimmed with the school hat-band. I saw the Office Manager, who knew the family quite well. He asked me a variety of questions – could I do shorthand and typing, or perhaps book-keeping? The answer to all these questions was "No!" Eventually, he asked me, quite kindly, if I really wanted a job with the Firm and I said that I didn't and that I wanted to return to school for another year. Doris, on being told about the interview, was appalled by my attitude, but the whole idea had been hers without any consideration for my wishes, so I was totally unrepentant. My rail season ticket duly arrived from Stafford, as always, and I returned to school for another year.

During that year, 1936-1937, I worked quite hard, played as much sport as I could get involved in and played my oboe at every opportunity. My annual performance on Speech Day was now an oboe solo, and I played 'Andante' by Mozart. For the second year in succession I was awarded 'Mrs. Lunt's Prize for Music', despite the fact that singing was still the only formal music taught in the school. A highlight in the year's activities was an invitation to tea at Miss Eastwood's house. I was also invited to take tea with Miss Eastwood and Miss Dale, the Headmistress, on the occasion of a visit to the school by an eminent inspector, whose name escapes me.

Events of historical significance took place during my last years at school. In May, 1935, and coinciding with School Certificate examinations, the Silver Jubilee of King George V and Queen Mary was celebrated. There were bonfires all over the country and we had one very close to home, on the 'Tump' beside Perry Park Road. Every girl in our school was presented with a copy of *The King's Grace* by John Buchan.

Although my parents had lived during the reigns of three monarchs – Queen Victoria, King Edward VII and King George V – we had known only one. King George V and Queen Mary were to us symbols of permanence and stability, conditions to which we never even considered the possibility of alternatives.

The death of King George V in January, 1936, was therefore a very disturbing occasion; our concept of permanence was shattered. The Prince of Wales immediately became King Edward VIII and, during the year which followed, the monarchy failed to establish for itself a positive identity. The

County High School for Girls, Stourbridge:
Forms VI Upper and Lower – June, 1937
(H.H. in front row, extreme left)

ultimate sense of instability fell on us all when, in December, 1936, King Edward VIII abdicated.

The coronation of King George VI and Queen Elizabeth on 12th May, 1937, restored our spirits considerably. There were many celebrations and one which I attended as a member of a party of Rangers – mostly school friends – was the London Girl Guides Coronation Rally at the Empire Stadium, Wembley, on 5th June, 1937. The Guest of Honour was H.R.H. The Princess Royal, who took the salute, and Lord and Lady Baden-Powell attended the celebrations. Music was played by the Band of the Royal Artillery. The new County of London Standard was presented to the County Commissioner for London, and this ceremony was followed by a parade of four thousand Rangers and Guides and almost two thousand Brownies. There were displays of Country Dancing and Physical Training, and an Overseas Pageant was presented. There were demonstrations of signalling, swimming, cycling, canoeing and riding on horseback, and the whole four-hour celebration concluded with a sing-song by six thousand Rangers, Guides and Rovers in the Arena, together with the whole vast audience. This event was overwhelmingly impressive to us, as schoolgirls; there had never been anything on that scale in our experience.

20 SUNDAY PICTORIAL, June 6, 1937.

PRINCES.
WITH THE
GIRL GUIDE

At the Empire Stadium, Wembley, 5th June, 1937. All London Girl Guides Grand Coronation Rally and Display. H.R.H. The Princess Royal, taking the salute

Yet the summer of 1937 was a time of mixed emotions. Celebrations related to the Coronation raised our spirits after the abdication; but, at the same time, we were depressed by another event, which happened uncomfortably near to England. The Spanish Civil War broke out during the summer of 1936. My annual verse for the school magazine reflects the impact that it made on us in our last year at school.

SUMMER 1937

A GENTLE breeze disturbs the summer air;
The sunlight, pouring from a cloudless sky,
Deepens the hue of tired flowers that lie,
Their beauty left, by summer's heat, less fair.

The happy children hurry out to play,
And frolic, chattering, across the fields;
They feel the joy that summer's beauty yields
From dawn till rest comes at the close of day.

At sunset, when the cool sea-breezes creep
Inward across the misty twilit land,
Then darkness over England takes command,
And veils her beauty, while in peace we sleep.

But what beyond this country's beauty rare?
Not peace, but iron and death—stupid warfare!

H. HUNTER, VI Upper.

The question of what I would do after leaving school arose again, with considerably more urgency than previously. Girls who were going to University or Training College were given guidance by the school; but no alternatives were suggested for those of us who were not going on to do further academic study.

A friend of mine, whose father was in the Civil Service, told me that she had decided to take a Civil Service examination and suggested that I should join her. We both submitted applications and attended the examination in Birmingham. The result was that she failed and I came top in the Birmingham District. Thus ended a good friendship!

I was duly notified that I had been appointed as Female Sorting Clerk and Telegraphist. Female I understood; Sorting Clerk I had no notion of; Telegraphist I hoped might involve using Morse Code which was my 'forte' in the Girl Guides. I had to present myself for work at the General Post Office, Pinfold Street, Birmingham, on the Monday following the last day of the school term.

I clearly remember the last day of term when my friends and I were saying our goodbyes to the Staff at school. We were asked: "When do you begin . . ." My friends were saying various dates in October; my own answer was "Next Monday!" I recall an unpleasant sensation of imminent doom in relation to the new experience which seemed threateningly close; in the event, it proved to be the most traumatic transition of my life.

Chapter 6:

DEPRESSION, DIRECTION AND DETERMINATION

On the fateful Monday morning of my awesome transition from schoolgirl to employee, I dressed appropriately in a sober tailored suit and made my way to Rowley Regis and Blackheath Station, which, though further from home than Old Hill, was the one we used for journeys to Birmingham to save a little on fare. The platform was full of people waiting for the same train and looking so weary and bored that they seemed to belong to a different world from mine. I wondered if I would ultimately look as bored as they did. They and I – I saw myself still as a separate entity – poured out of the train at Snow Hill Station. I walked along Colmore Row and arrived at the General Post Office, Pinfold Street entrance. It looked a dark forbidding building from the outside: it proved to be worse within.

General Post Office, Birmingham

Council House, Birmingham

I was directed by a commissionaire to the Telegraph School. I walked up several flights of narrow, dusty concrete stairs, and along corridors, and eventually I arrived on the top floor of the building. I approached the door marked Telegraph School with some trepidation. However, I was welcomed by a pleasant jovial man, Mr. Joe Harkness, who introduced me to his assistant, Miss Gossage, a brisk, lively lady. Together, they created a busy but friendly atmosphere in the school. Mr. Harkness proved to be the one person in 'Telegraphs' with whom one could discuss or share a problem.

The overwhelming impression was one of incredibly noisy activity in a cramped space. There were long tables with several teleprinters on each and most of them were staffed by two girls of about my own age. A teleprinter was a very noisy and continuously throbbing machine, electrically driven and almost totally enclosed in a hollow iron casing. There was a keyboard, with a typewriter-like layout of letters – 'qwerty' style – but with capitals only. Figures and letters shared the same keys and a split space-bar facilitated changing between them. A few keys carried special signs. On the left side of the machine was a space through which gummed paper tape emerged. The teleprinter could be switched to produce type on the tape in its own machine or it could be switched to print on the tape of a machine in another town. In that case, there was no record of what was being typed except on the tape in the distant town, so accuracy in touch-typing (teleprinter style) was essential. The machines in the school were all switched to print on their own tape, for practice purposes. My hope of using Morse Code was dashed; it had gone out of use several years previously!

My first task was therefore to become an accurate and speedy touch-typist. Then I had to learn the conventional format of a telegram heading – serial number, type of message (greetings, telegraph money order or other), time handed in, office of origin and number of words. All figures in a message had to be signalled twice and checked for correspondence, to make doubly sure that no error had occurred.

After basic word-practice, one progressed to telegrams. A pile of these was placed on the sloping front of the teleprinter. After transmission, each message was marked with the time of completion and signed by the operator who then transferred it to a tray for 'dead' messages, or 'gone-ons' as they were called, on top of the teleprinter. The messages on tape had to be gummed on to official forms in a specified format, signed, and passed on for circulation.

Mr. Harkness told a tale – undoubtedly a fictitious one – to illustrate the need for accuracy in signalling figures. A butcher sent a telegram ordering '4 1/4 pigs' from a supplier. (That was the conventional way of signalling ' four quarter-pigs'.) A mistake in transmission resulted in the arrival on New Street Station of 414 (four hundred and fourteen) pigs! Mr. Harkness was a good teacher, stressing important points by relating anecdotes.

We were allowed three months for training, during which time we were paid twelve shillings and sixpence weekly. A further three months were allowed if training had not been completed, during which payment was fifteen shillings weekly. When qualification was achieved and one was allowed into the Telegraph Office to do 'live' work, payment was increased to one pound twelve shillings and sixpence weekly, and annual increments amounting to two shillings and sixpence weekly were awarded.

'Qualification' meant the ability to signal sixty telegrams in an hour with fewer than five errors overall, and to receive, gum on to forms in the prescribed manner, check, time and sign eighty telegrams per hour. I qualified in three months and was promoted to 'live' work in the Telegraph Office.

This was an enormous office, occupying virtually the whole of the top floor of the 'old' Post Office building. It had a roof which was made largely of glass, which, together with plenty of windows, made it pleasantly light. However, that was its only pleasant feature. The noise in that room was overwhelming.

Entering the Telegraph Office through a revolving door, one arrived in a 'walkway' which ran the full length of the Office. To one side were two clocks which one had to punch with a Duty Number to register one's time of arrival each morning and departure at the end of a shift. Lateness of two minutes or more in arrival had to be explained in writing in answer to a 'report', and an unsatisfactory reason for lateness was penalised by deduction from weekly payment.

Further along were notice-boards containing a list of about two hundred Duty Numbers with details of the time of the shift and the daily programme for each Duty. Shifts were eight hours: 8 to 4, 9 to 5, 10 to 6, 11 to 7, or 12 to 8, on six days of every week. Some duties were known as 'long and short' which meant 10 to 8 on Monday, Wednesday and Friday and 8 to 2 on Tuesday, Thursday and Saturday. The reverse of this, which most girls disliked, was 'short and long' which was 8 to 2 on Monday, Wednesday and Friday and 10 to 8 on Tuesday, Thursday and Saturday. In addition, some Sunday duties of at least six hours were demanded, and these and any hours of overtime allocated were paid at rates of one or two shillings an hour, depending on one's normal rate of payment.

A break of fifteen minutes precisely was allowed each day during morning and afternoon, and lunchtime was exactly forty minutes to ensure that meals could only be taken in the canteen, which was in the newer Post Office building, reached by crossing the bridge over Hill Street. From there one could get out, for the few available minutes after a meal, on to the roof of

Victoria Square, Birmingham, in 1938, showing column erected in 1937 to mark the Coronation of King George VI and Queen Elizabeth. Photograph taken by the author from the roof of the 'new' Post Office at the top of Hill Street.

that building, which provided the only accessible 'fresh' air. The exact times when these breaks might be taken were specified on the Duty Sheet which had to be adhered to meticulously. Punctuality was a priority throughout the office; no one was allowed to leave a circuit until her 'relief' had arrived to occupy her chair.

At right-angles to the 'walkway' were long tables separated by aisles. The tables were wide enough to accommodate a double row of teleprinters, back to back, and between these was a channel containing a moving band which ran the length of the table. There were about nine or ten such double tables, each with about five teleprinters on either side. Every teleprinter was electrically linked to a similar one sited in a distant town, the code for that town being indicated on the top of the machine. Some major towns had two or more circuits connecting them with Birmingham. London (coded TS, meaning Threadneedle Street) usually had four or five circuits open.

Busy circuits were manned by two people, one to send and one to receive messages; less busy ones were attended by only one person. The least busy towns were connected to switchboards which allowed the telegraphist to plug into each town as a light showed that it was calling for attention. These switchboard points were grouped together in the 'ancillary' section of the office. Before signalling messages, one had to check that the connection with the distant town was correct by pressing the 'answer back' key, which produced the appropriate code on tape, confirming the connection.

The person receiving messages would gum the tape on to forms (there was a brass roller revolving in water for gumming tape at every teleprinter circuit), sign each message and stamp it with the time of receipt by means of a 'blick' electric timer (or by hand if the circuit had no 'blick'), and drop it on edge on to the moving band in the channel in front of her, whence it would be conveyed to the end of the table and would fall on to a larger band travelling the length of the office. This band deposited all telegrams at a central area called 'circulation'.

Here, a number of people were engaged in sorting all telegrams according to their destinations, writing on them the code for the circuit at which they would be signalled, and slotting them on to moving bands travelling in the opposite direction, from which they were deposited on the table where the circuit to that destination was sited. A messenger boy collected them and distributed them without delay along the two tables for which he was responsible, placing them on the in-tray on top of the appropriate teleprinter. The telegraphist would number the messages, signal them, 'blick' them with the time of sending, and store them in the tray provided for 'gone-ons'. The now 'dead' telegrams were collected by other messenger boys who took them to a central point where they were sorted and stored in case future reference might be needed.

The people on 'circulation' were usually older and more experienced telegraphists who knew to which central town each telegram had to be signalled for distribution. Any towns or villages not known could be looked up in an index showing circulation centres and the places to which they had distribution facilities.

Speed and accuracy were the essential elements in every operation throughout the entire Telegraph Office, as every telegram had to be received by its addressee within minutes of its handing-in time. There were always engineers on hand, ready to deal immediately with teleprinter or other electrical faults, or with messages stuck to moving bands which sometimes had to be stopped momentarily for their retrieval. There was also a senior male supervisor to every double table of teleprinters, always alert to deal with any problem which might arise.

Next door to the teleprinter office was the Telephone Section where telegrams were received directly from the public or telephoned to addressees whose telephone number was in the address. As one became more experienced, one had duties which included a spell of time in 'phones', which a number of us disliked intensely. All the supervisors were women; they had long service either in Telegraphs or at Telephone House and they assumed an air of superiority which was most oppressive. I disliked having to wear headphones for long periods, and the whole procedure in 'phones' was to me even more monotonous than that of the main room.

Work in the Telegraph Office demanded continuous alert concentration, but when one had become accustomed to it the only section which demanded any mental effort was 'circulation', to which I was more and more frequently drafted as time went on.

The people in the office were mainly girls a little older than myself. There were also some elderly ladies who had been on the 'temporary' staff since their employment during World War I about twenty years earlier. They could not become 'established' staff because they had not entered by examination. There were also a few male telegraphists, again mostly elderly, who dealt largely with the circulation of foreign telegrams and with queries, and who did overnight shifts. Some of them liked to be given overtime duties in the daytime, though occasionally a man would fall asleep; it was always one of the girls who was called upon to clear up the yards of tape and piles of accumulated telegrams in double-quick time.

There was an even more boring job which we were sometimes scheduled to do, in the 'Wireless Records' office. There, we were presented with a list of people who had failed to renew their licences at the appropriate time and we had to address a printed postcard to each of them, demanding payment. The only saving grace of this duty was that the office was quiet!

It was permissible – though not always easy – to exchange duties with another person, and I often needed to do so in order to get to orchestral rehearsals in Stourbridge or to lessons with Lucy. I managed reasonably well, though with some difficulty, to keep my music going through this period.

The philosophy of work in those days was to 'find a safe job and stick to it'. I had a safe job, but I had no intention of staying in it for a moment longer than was necessary. There was no future except the prospect of continuing to handle many hundreds of telegrams daily – for life! Yet I found myself unable to think of a good alternative.

In the summer of 1938 when I had been at the Post Office for just one long tedious year, political events conspired to make working in Telegraphs even more oppressive. A political 'crisis' developed, created by Germany, and for a time, war seemed imminent. One day we returned to the Telegraph Office to find all the windows and the glass of the ceiling painted with a dense black paint. This was said to be necessary in case of war and air raids. The crisis passed – temporarily, at least – but the black paint remained. We worked in artificial light from that time onward.

Holidays from the office were very precious. Bank holidays were extremely busy and were never taken; instead, one accumulated a collection of 'odd days', usually taken in October. The busiest days of the year were August Bank Holiday, when it seemed that all the world had gone on holiday and had 'arrived safely – weather good' or some such message, and Christmas Day, when an incredible number of people sent Greetings telegrams to each other. On these days, it was commonplace to be signalling eighty or ninety messages per hour and receiving a hundred or more.

On Christmas Days there was no public transport and I had to cycle to the office. One Christmas Day, when we had had unusually heavy snow during the previous night, I set out with my bicycle in deep untreated snow, hoping that conditions might be better when I reached the main Hagley Road into Birmingham, a mile or so from home. They were not, and I was exhausted by my efforts, so I returned home. After a few days, all the people who had failed to arrive for work on that Christmas Day were served with 'reports', on which we had to explain the precise reasons for our absence. No fines were imposed on that occasion, as far as I remember!

I spent my annual fortnight's holiday in 1938 on my bicycle. Doris and I had each bought new 'Sunbeam' cycles at a reduced rate (about £6 each) through the Firm, and prior to my leaving school we had both cycled at weekends with the Firm's Cycling Club where we learned good cycling manners. We rode in pairs, with an experienced rider in front and another behind. When a car approached from in front, the leader called "Line up!" and the outside riders fell behind, all along the line. Conversely, when a car

Hilda Hunter

approached from behind, the back rider called "Line up!" and the outside riders slotted in, in front of their partners. This code was very rigidly adhered to, and there were never any difficulties or accidents. Two members of the club, man and wife, rode a tandem bicycle; he rode in front, and his wife rode behind, knitting his socks as she pedalled! We would ride out about twenty-five miles, eat ham and eggs, at a Cyclists' Touring Club hostelry, and then return home.

Once a year, we joined with other Cycling Clubs in a visit to Meriden Cross – considered to be the centre of England – to join in a service, organised by the Cyclists' Touring Club, to commemorate the cyclists who had lost their lives in the First World War.

Doris and I arranged holiday dates together in 1938 in order to do a cycling tour in Wales. We were both in fairly good form, and the tour was a great success. Supper, bed and breakfast cost approximately five shillings in those days!

Proposed Tour.
27.6.38 to 9.7.38.

							B.F.	312	
Home	to	Kidderminster	12 miles	Aberystwyth	to	Machynlleth		20	miles
K.	to	Tenbury Wells	17 ..	M.	..	Aberdovey		11	..
T.W.	..	Leominster	11 ..	A.	..	Towyn		4	..
L.	..	Kington	14 ..	T.	..	Dolgelley		20	..
K.	..	New Radnor	7 ..	D.	..	Barmouth		10	..
N.R.	..	Builth Wells	13 ..	B.	..	Harlech		11	..
B.W.	..	Rhayader	14 ..	H.	..	Maentwrog		10	..
R.	..	Llanguriq	9 ..	M.	..	Penrhyndeudraeth		5	..
L.	..	Pontrwydd	13 ..	P.	..	Beddgelert		8	..
P.	..	Tregarron	20 ..	B.	..	Caernarvon		13	..
T.	..	Lampeter	11 ..	C.	..	Llanberis		8	..
L.	..	Carmarthen	22 ..	L.	..	Capel Curig		10	..
C.	..	St. Clears	9 ..	C.C.	..	Betws-y-coed		5	..
S.C.	..	Red Roses	6 ..	B.	..	Druid		19	..
R.R.	..	Beqelly	7 ..	D.	..	Bala		9	..
B.	..	Pembroke	10 ..	B.	..	Dolgelley		19	..
P.	..	Milford Haven	10 ..	D.	..	Machynlleth		16	..
M.H.	..	Haverfordwest	7 ..	M.	..	Caersws		22	..
H.	..	St. Davids	20 ..	C.	..	Newtown		6	..
S.D.	..	Goodwick	20 ..	N.	..	Kerry		3	..
G.	..	Fishguard	2 ..	K.	..	Church Stoke		9	..
F.	..	Cardigan	19 ..	C.S.	..	Lydham		5	..
C.	..	Synod	16 ..	L.	..	Craven Arms		8	..
S.	..	Aberayron	7 ..	C.A.	..	Much Wenlock		20	..
A.	..	Aberystwyth	16 ..	M.W.	..	Bridgnorth		10	..
				B.	..	Stourbridge		15	..
		C.F.	312 ..	S.	..	Home		5	..
								613	miles.

Proposed Cycling Tour, 1938

I sometimes travelled by bus to Birmingham as a change from the train, and sometimes I cycled. If the weather was foggy – as it frequently was – I could make the seven-mile journey more quickly by bicycle than by public transport.

For some months, life went on with customary monotony. If one were scheduled in the early morning for a circuit such as Grimsby, Milford Haven or Aberdeen, there would be frantic activity as fish prices came tumbling out on tape. These had to be carefully checked against the repetition of figures and any failure in correspondence had to be queried in the approved style. Later in the day these circuits would slow down and be switched to ancillary. If there were events such as race meetings or other sporting fixtures, the circuits involved would be intensely active and sometimes extra circuits had to be brought into use. Often there were sheets of press reports to send or receive; these sometimes served to relieve the monotony of work but the stress was continuous.

During the summer months of 1939, telegraphic traffic increased substantially, especially on the London circuits. Press reports were frequent and long, and coded messages became commonplace. Messages relating to the Armed Forces increased in number and complexity and there was an unaccustomed anxiety throughout the entire office. Tension – and workload – had already increased to crisis proportions by the time that war was declared on 3rd September, 1939. I was on duty that Sunday, and I clearly remember the anxiety among all the Staff. Many of the older people had already experienced a war and knew of its horrors; the younger people were anxious for the menfolk in their lives, who would inevitably be called upon for service.

First Aid and Nursing courses had already taken place, and qualified First Aiders had always to wear their St. John Armbands and A.R.P. badges to make them distinguishable in a crisis. Gas masks had to be carried everywhere, and instructions were issued for speedy evacuation of the Telegraph Office (extremely vulnerable on the top floor of the building and with areas of glass in its roof) and for resumption of work in the temporary office in the basement in the event of Air Raid activity. Tension continued to mount and so did the quantity of work. Before long, everyone was compelled to do three hours' overtime daily, either at the beginning or the end of their normal shift, so we were working six eleven-hour days weekly and six or more hours almost every Sunday. I used my bicycle more and more frequently for my journeys to work, in order to have some time in the open air.

At home, the toolhouse had been tidied and made habitable as an air raid shelter. It had electric light, and we kept a supply of candles and torches in case the power failed. It also had a small electric fire and blackout curtains. We became accustomed to a routine of cooking a meal in the kitchen and carrying it down to the toolhouse before the air raid sirens sounded.

Father and Doris were in 'reserved occupations' at Stewarts and Lloyds and my work also was 'reserved'. Mary was still at school. Father did some firewatching duties and, later, Doris joined the National Fire Service and did some night duties, manning the telephone at the local Fire Station.

My working hours at the GPO, and travelling times, were so long that I was getting exhausted. On winter days I left home and returned there in darkness and worked all day in artificial light. In addition, we would get up in the night when air raid sirens sounded and spend hours in the toolhouse. Eventually I transferred my bed to the toolhouse and slept there, damp though it was, for months.

The strain of working at the GPO and sometimes travelling home through air raids began to affect my health seriously, and the consensus of family opinion was that I would be better if I resigned from the Post Office and went to work at Stewarts and Lloyds. This proposition was not attractive to me but it was obviously sensible, and permissible because I would be moving to another 'reserved' occupation. So arrangements were made with the Firm, and on 11th November, 1940, just before my twenty-first birthday, I began work in the offices at Coombs Wood.

Stewarts and Lloyds had established within itself a firm called 'New Crown Forgings' to deal with all its work on munitions. A man had been appointed to write an account of the work of NCF, and his book had to be typed. I was given the job of doing this as my first assignment. His writing was appalling – very cramped, shapeless and difficult to decipher, especially as the subject matter was unfamiliar. To compound my misery I was put to work in Doris's office. She wanted me to learn 'correct' typewriter fingering, based on a different set of 'guide keys'. This I positively refused to do.

I had been asked by the Firm to learn shorthand, under Doris's guidance, but teaching within a family is rarely successful. Doris wanted me to develop speed before I had sufficient knowledge of shorthand outlines, which would have meant my practising mistakes. This, I knew, was bad teaching technique and I obstinately refused to comply. Arguments followed, and trying to learn in this situation was sheer misery and a dismal failure on my part. During this time she was domineering in the extreme (and I was unco-operative), and there were many times when I felt that even the Post Office might have been preferable!

There was some advantage in working for the Firm, however. The Stourbridge Orchestra had moved its rehearsals from Friday evenings to Sunday afternoons to avoid the problems of travelling in black-out conditions. I could now go to rehearsals since I was no longer involved in Sunday working, and I resumed my orchestral activities with enthusiasm. I also managed to fit in fairly frequent lessons with Lucy.

There was a great deal of amateur music-making around this time. Amateur orchestras did everything in their power to beat wartime conditions (such as blackout, loss of venues for rehearsals, transport problems caused by shortage of petrol and of public transport, and of course, loss of players to the Forces), and to continue their performances in the interests of boosting the morale of the general public.

One such orchestra was based at Reddal Hill, Old Hill, and I was frequently invited to play in its concerts. It was conducted by William Perks, who had an amiable temperament, and a gift for helping players to give their best possible musical performances. He was a modest man who probably underrated his own musicianship. He was always most appreciative of one's playing and of the loyalty of his orchestra.

Mr. Perks gave a series of concerts in the Majestic Theatre, Cradley Heath, during the War years. The concerts were always given on Sunday evenings, to permit of rehearsal with soloists and the full orchestra on the day of the concert. The Sundays chosen were always at full moon, to cause players and audience the least possible inconvenience from the wartime black-out! The works performed included Verdi's *Requiem* which I remember particularly because one soloist sang in Latin and another sang a particularly banal English translation! Mr. Perks always engaged the best of soloists, among whom I remember especially Kathleen Ferrier. She had the most gloriously rich contralto voice; but also she had a friendly manner and a keen sense of humour. Whereas some soloists were inclined to remain aloof from the orchestra, Kathleen was invariably pleasant and friendly with everybody.

During the war and for a time afterwards, town halls and concert halls were unheated, and members of the orchestra had the dual problem of cold, stiff fingers, and the difficulty of keeping instruments sufficiently warm to play in tune. It was quite usual for ladies in long black dresses to be wearing warm pullovers and skirts beneath them. Equally, woodwind players could be seen cuddling their instruments, during rests in the music, trying to keep them warm and capable of being played up to pitch.

When the NCF book was completed, and by chance on my twenty-first birthday (which passed unnoticed except that we had tinned fruit for tea at home that day), I was moved into a small office of six typists who shared the work of Buying Office and Cost Office typing. I was allocated to the Cost Office, for which one had to copy Cost Sheets. These were large sheets of figures and details, which had to be fitted into tiny squares and columns.

Several copies had to be made simultaneously by using carbon paper, and it was always difficult to get the information on the bottom copies aligned with the sheets, because the cylindrical typewriter roller misplaced them in relation to each other. My companion in this work was a pleasant enough person, but she was an incorrigible chatterbox. I found this very wearing and eventually I asked to be transferred to another office.

I knew that the Cashier needed an assistant. He was an elderly gentleman whom I knew and respected, and I was allowed to move into his office and to become responsible with him for everything concerned with wages for weekly-paid Staff. He was very much interested in music, and we talked a great deal about it. Life was considerably more interesting and less harassing from that time onward.

I had approached Lucy about the prospect of my taking a diploma examination in oboe playing. She was not particularly keen on the idea but she did not raise any serious objections and she worked with me on the syllabus. I passed the examination and was awarded the L.R.A.M. Diploma in Oboe Playing in 1943. By way of celebration, I took Mary for a day out in Wolverhampton, a town I had not previously visited, though I had passed through its railway station en route for holidays in Aberystwyth. I had no idea of the importance which those two towns were to assume in my future musical activities!

It was about this time that Lucy was faced with a crisis in her professional life. Her very great friend, Leslie Heward, who had conducted the CBO since 1930, and who had been seriously ill for some time, died in 1943. This was an intensely sad time for Lucy, as it was for many other musicians whose admiration for Leslie Heward's musical integrity was unbounded.

A period followed during which the appointment of a new conductor for the CBO was under discussion, as was the prospect of establishing the orchestra for the first time on a permanent basis. Eventually, George Weldon was appointed conductor, and for the orchestra a period of internal turbulence ensued.

Another change was the separation of the BBC Midland Light Orchestra from the CBO. Prior to 1944 the two orchestras had co-operated and shared musicians; but with the establishment of the CBO as a permanent orchestra, such mutual help was neither feasible nor necessary.

Auditions were held, not only for aspiring new members of the CBO but also among existing members, who, having given excellent service to the orchestra through extremely difficult times, felt this to be an indignity to which they should not be subjected.

Lucy felt that, having satisfied Sir Thomas Beecham, Sir Adrian Boult, and other eminent conductors who of course included Leslie Heward, she

should not be required to be judged by audition. She had experienced the
new régime, and had realised that her musical integrity would not be
sustainable within it. There has to be, in an orchestra, a rapport between
conductor and players, and Lucy knew that, for her, this essential element
was missing. She applied for, and obtained, an appointment as Principal
Oboist in one of the full-time orchestras in the north of England.

Lucy Vincent
Photo: H. Hunter

For me, as for her other pupils, this was very sad news. Lucy had a wonderful and unique personality, and we all loved her and admired her musicianship and total musical integrity. She was quiet and unpretentious in manner, but with strict and unwavering loyalty to high principles, in music and in all aspects of life. She was warm and sympathetic; but if her principles were challenged, she would be aggressive in their protection.

Whilst she lived in Birmingham, Lucy was also Teacher of Oboe at the Birmingham and Midland Institute School of Music, though at the time of her move to the North, there were no oboe pupils there. She still taught a small number of pupils at her home.

Amateur orchestras around the Midlands were in the habit of inviting members of the CBO to play in their concerts, and Lucy had booked several such engagements.

She discussed with me my plans for my future, knowing, as well as I did, that my heart was not in commerce but irrevocably in music. She lectured me – in the kindest possible manner – about my need to be positive and not self-effacing; to acknowledge my ability in various directions, and especially not to underestimate my musical potential but to develop it fully.

Lucy asked me if I would take on the work to which she was at present committed, and when I agreed to do so she approached the various individuals concerned. They all trusted her judgement without question, and accepted her recommendation. The Principal of Birmingham School of Music, Dr. Alan Blackall, appointed me as Teacher of Oboe, and I continued when, on his retirement, he was succeeded by Dr. Christopher Edmunds. I spent many happy years teaching at the School, despite the fact that the building was old-fashioned and not at all appropriate to a developing School of Music. There was no sound-proofing whatever and one could be teaching an individual student, whom one was exhorting to listen intently to details of sound, when suddenly, next door, a full orchestral rehearsal would begin! Yet the atmosphere was very friendly and pleasant.

At the same time, I inherited a very special private pupil from Lucy. He was a young boy about eleven years old, very pleasant and courteous in manner, very alert and outstandingly musical. His name was Neil Black. I was invited by his mother to teach him at their home, where I was always made most welcome. Neil's parents were wonderfully supportive of him – and of me, too – and I thoroughly enjoyed the long lessons we had – as I know Neil did. He was totally responsive and hard-working, full of good humour yet wholly dedicated to his music. I taught him until he went to Rugby School, and then during his school holidays. During that time, Neil had been accepted into the National Youth Orchestra. Though it was then in its infancy, he gained very valuable experience of orchestral playing and repertoire.

At Oxford, Neil was highly regarded as a musician and especially on account of his performances in works by J. S. Bach, conducted by Dr. Thomas Armstrong. After graduating in history he moved to London where he soon established an outstanding reputation in orchestral, chamber music and solo performances. Sir Thomas Armstrong had, by that time, been appointed Principal of the Royal Academy of Music, London, and he invited Neil to join his Staff as Professor of Oboe. From 1970 until fairly recently, he was Principal Oboist in the English Chamber Orchestra.

Neil Back, Dr. Percy M. Young and myself
(Summer Music School at St. Andrews, 1949)

In 1989 Neil was awarded the honour of OBE for Services to Music. He established for himself an international reputation for artistry in playing and total musical integrity. Yet he has never lost his courteous and generous nature, nor his keen sense of humour. He is very much admired and is, indeed, the 'beloved musician'.

Neil's competence as an oboist overtook and outpaced mine many years ago. I can now only – but with enormous pleasure – bathe in a modicum of reflected glory!

Neil Black (1997)

Photo: *Janice Black*

The professional concert engagements in Worcester, Shrewsbury and Wolverhampton, which Lucy passed on to me proved to be the first of many which came my way in those and other towns. Soon, I found myself in a situation where office work and music were becoming incompatible and I needed expert advice.

For some time I had been having piano lessons with Frank Edwards, and lately I had transferred from piano to organ to widen my keyboard experience. Frank Edwards was organist at Halesowen Parish Church and it was there that I had my lessons and did my practice. The blackout was still in force, so a torch was essential equipment, but the church was always open and there was no fear of disturbance in those days.

Mother, Mary and I regularly attended Evensong at Halesowen on Sundays and we always enjoyed Mr. Edwards' organ playing and the singing of the choir which he trained. Occasionally I played an oboe solo with him, during the service.

Anyone doing organ practice had to sign a practice register and periodically pay at the rate of sixpence an hour as a contribution towards electricity consumed by the organ. My name alternated with that of W. S. Ingley, whom I did not know at that time, but who came into my life some years later.

Meanwhile, at Stewarts and Lloyds I had been selected to attend a Business Management Course on one afternoon weekly at Birmingham Technical College. I was taken there in the Works car each week. Some of the lectures I could follow, but for others I had insufficient background knowledge to enable me to understand them thoroughly, which left me somewhat confused. I did, however, find it very stimulating to be placed in a learning situation once again, but I wished that the subject matter had been of more interest to me.

The Cashier fell ill and was on sick leave for a considerable time. During his absence I carried on dealing with weekly-paid Staff wages on my own, and the Office Manager took over monthly-salaried payments. It was then that the Inland Revenue introduced the 'Pay-as-you-earn' system of income tax. I had to reorganise the whole manner of tax deductions and devise a new layout for the wages books. This was a challenge which I enjoyed and dealt with successfully.

The Cashier returned to work only briefly and soon he retired. He was replaced by a man for whom I had very little respect or liking – a pompous man of small stature and compensating self-importance – but he was reasonably amiable towards me – understandably so because he was not yet familiar with the work he was appointed to do, and he needed my guidance to some extent. Again, I saw nothing attractive to look forward to; I had arrived at another 'dead end'.

I decided to talk to Frank Edwards about the conflict between my work at Stewarts and Lloyds and my increasing work as a professional musician. I asked his advice on how I might best try to resolve my predicament. This was in the late Spring of 1945. He was a very wise and experienced man, and he put his advice in terms of organ playing.

He said that an organist could not progress from being a village organist to becoming a cathedral organist, and that, in music, one had to step in at the level which one wanted to achieve. It followed, he said, that one had to become fully qualified for work at that level. He said that I ought, therefore, to go to University for three years and work for a music degree. I said that I had to consider the family, to whom I made a financial contribution, and that I could not give up earning an income for three years. He said that I would still have my income from musical activities, and that there was also the possibility of my getting a grant to help with finances.

My first step would have to be to get a matriculation qualification, which had eluded me during schooldays. Mr. Edwards knew that a 'Matriculation Examination for People of Mature Years' had recently been announced, mainly for the benefit of returning Servicemen, but he knew no details, so he advised me to see the Headmaster of Halesowen Grammar School whom he knew well. Mr. Mander was most helpful in giving me details about the examination, and about how and where to apply for a grant.

Naturally, when I told my parents about my discussions, they were considerably shaken, since they had always believed in the theory of getting a 'safe' job and keeping it. Their first thought was about income – or rather, lack of it – and I assured them that I could get help in that direction. To their credit, when they had recovered from the initial shock, they once again gave way to experienced advice and superior wisdom, and they cautiously agreed that I should go ahead and get all the information I could.

By this time, the War in Europe was clearly grinding inexorably to its conclusion. Ex-Servicemen were returning home and people in 'reserved' occupations were being permitted to become mobile again.

The date of the 'Mature Matriculation' examination was announced, and I asked to see the Office Manager and Cashier of Stewarts and Lloyds together. I told them of my intended plans and asked for time off work to attend the examination. There were raised eyebrows, and I was reminded that I had been privileged to attend the Business Management Course. I replied that I appreciated that, but the Course had not only whetted my appetite for further study but had shown me that my career was not in business management. The Cashier (the little man) said: "Suppose you fail this examination – what will you expect to do then?" Lucy's advice shot into my mind but I was still very surprised to hear myself saying: "I have no intention of failing, so the question is hypothetical!" I was granted two days off work to take the examination.

My French was decidedly rusty after eight years of neglect, so I went to see my school French mistress, Miss Eunice Wells. She was her usual generous self and she gave me a series of lessons at her home. I took the examination, and to my great relief, I soon heard that I had passed it.

The next hurdle was an interview with Professor Jack Westrup at the Barber Institute of Fine Arts, Birmingham University. Although he was very amiable, I felt as I left that I had no hope of acceptance and I walked disconsolately for several miles of my homeward journey. However, my fears proved groundless, for, several days later, I received a letter from Professor Westrup, who had examined the work in harmony which I had done for Frank Edwards. On the strength of that, together with my oboe playing, he offered me a place in the Music Degree Course, beginning in October, 1945. Not only that, but on the merit of my oboe playing, I had also been awarded a small 'Barber Scholarship'!

Some days later, I was informed that I had been granted an amount of £26 per year towards books, by Staffordshire Education Committee – my faithful friends! A further grant of £10 per year was given to me by the Foyle Trust of Birmingham.

I was happier than I had been for years – though still a little apprehensive because it was eight years since I had left school. I knew that the other students on the course would have come straight out of school, having passed Higher School Certificate Music which I had never done. However, nothing was going to daunt me now! On 31st August, 1945, I said goodbye to Stewarts and Lloyds – who, to be fair, had come to my rescue twice, enabling me to leave the Post Office at crisis point in 1940, and lending me their little high-pitch oboe on which I first learned to play. I turned my back on industry and commerce and launched myself wholly into the somewhat amorphous world of professional music!

Chapter 7:

RENAISSANCE AND REFORMATION

On a beautiful October day in 1945 I presented myself at the Barber Institute of Fine Arts, Edgbaston, Birmingham, ready and keen to begin my new life. There was only one problem – I was a day early! I returned next day and I remember, even now, the peculiar feeling of unreality about the situation – could this really be happening to me? Well, it could, and I was actually there! Despite the misgivings which from time to time flashed through my mind, I knew deep down that I would do everything possible to make a success of my new way of life, in which age-disadvantage and the eight years since school might well be outweighed by the advantages of experience.

Postcard commemorating the opening of Birmingham University by King Edward VII and Queen Alexandra in July, 1909

The Barber Institute of Fine Arts, Birmingham University in 1945
Photo: Eric Merriman

Professor Jack Westrup – 1945

Photo: Eric Merriman

There were eight of us in the First Year Music Course. After introductions to the Music Staff and the Department of Music, we had to go into Town to the University building in Edmund Street to settle details of subsidiary subjects with tutors and finally with the Registrar. We also did some shopping for books.

Birmingham University: Five Professors of Music

Left:
The late
Sir Granville Bantock
1908–1934

Right:
The late
Sir Edward Elgar
1905–1908

The late Professor
Victor Hely-Hutchinson
1934–1944

Left:
The late Professor
J. A. Westrup
1944–1947

Right:
The late Professor
Anthony Lewis
1947–1968

First Year Music Students – 1945
(H.H. is on extreme right)

Photo: Eric Merriman

First, Second and Third Year Music Students
with Lecturer Miss Hannah Jones – 1945
(H.H. is back row, second from right)

One of the Music students, Mary Randall, had already successfully completed a two-year course in the Education Department at Edmund Street, and she knew exactly where to go and what to do. S   he was most kind and helpful to me and we became very good friends. We followed identical courses throughout our three years and were always together.

Mary had the most beautiful soprano voice, and on many occasions we gave performances in which voice and oboe were prominent. One memorable performance was of Bach's *Cantata 140, Sleepers, wake!* in which Mary sang solo soprano and I played the oboe obbligato. It was sheer joy to play with her. She also gave a wonderful performance of Purcell's *The Blessed Virgin's Expostulation* – a dramatic work which required a wide range of expressive and sensitive singing, at which Mary excelled. We enjoyed working together, and Professor Westrup always gave us generous support and encouragement.

It took longer than I had imagined to get details of courses sorted out. There was much walking around the building at Edmund Street, finding specific members of Staff, and queuing for individual interviews. The process extended over several days, during which we were also required to attend Music lectures at the Barber Institute. We were frequently catching trams up or down the Bristol Road to keep appointments on both sites. Mary and I did subsidiary English, and all English lectures took place at Edmund Street, so the tram journeys became a part of life.

I also had to re-organise some of my teaching activities at the School of Music, which, fortunately, was less than five minutes' walk from the University in Edmund Street. When concert dates were offered to me I had to consider carefully how I could slot them into my timetable without prejudicing my studies. I also continued my piano lessons with Frank Edwards, though I had insufficient time to keep up organ study. I continued to live at home, and my journeys were made mainly by bus. Sometimes I cycled, to make a speedier journey cross-country to the Barber Institute.

I had been a student for about two weeks when, during a lecture in musical history, I had a most uncomfortable feeling. I habitually wore a suit and shirt blouse (clothing coupons were still in force!), and on this particular day I was wearing a high-necked blouse with 'trubenised' (slightly stiffened) collar and a tie. The collar became noticeably tighter as the lecture progressed. When it ended I returned home, and on my way through Blackheath I decided to call in at my Doctor's surgery. He examined my neck and asked if I felt ill. I said I didn't – just tired – and he said: "You will, tomorrow and I'll call and see you then. Go home and go to bed – you've got bi-lateral mumps!" Mumps at the age of twenty-five is not funny – in fact it is decidedly unpleasant, and I did feel very ill. I think, though, that the first two weeks of my new way of life had been more stressful than I had realised, and two weeks of mumps gave me vital recovery time from that stress. I was back 'on course' at the end of a fortnight and resumed all my activities.

As the University course became a more familiar routine, the stress element was reduced somewhat. There was still a fair amount of tram-chasing to do, but one became more accustomed to using time more efficiently. In addition to lectures, there were Friday lunch-time concerts at the Barber Institute. Sometimes we were audience, but we were often performers, and rehearsals had to be fitted in to our busy schedule. In addition, Mary and I were asked to organise a series of Monday lunch-time concerts at Edmund Street, and these became quite popular and were well supported by students and Staff. The series of Barber Evening Concerts was initiated in 1945 by Professor Westrup, and these gave us wonderful opportunities of hearing outstanding performances by eminent musicians.

In the summer of 1946, first year examinations took place. Playing 'figured harmony at the keyboard' was to me a new and difficult skill which I have never really come to terms with. Neither was I capable of completing counterpoint exercises within the allotted time. Oddly enough, my good friend Mary had identical problems, and Professor Westrup advised us both to transfer from the B.Mus. course to the course for B.A. in Music. In our second year we both studied Music, English and French, then in our third year, French, Philosophy and Psychology. It is interesting to me, looking back, to observe that this particular combination of subjects has proved more appropriate in my subsequent studies than the B.Mus. course might have been, though it could be argued that this is the 'chicken and the egg' syndrome! The fact remains that I enjoyed these subjects very much indeed.

We attended a most interesting series of lectures in our second year. They were on Acoustics, and were given by Dr. Martin Johnson of the Department of Physics, who was also Chairman of the University Music Society when I was its Secretary.

During my third year, I was feeling the strain of all my activities, and I discussed this with Dr. Johnson, and said that I must give up my work on the Committee of the Music Society. He was quite concerned, and he must have conveyed his concern to the Senior Women's Tutor, who asked me to see her. She knew of my outside activities, and suggested that I should give up my teaching at the School of Music. She was surprised when I refused. I had to point out that my University course was intended, not to interrupt my teaching, but to enable me to do it better!

During the three years at Birmingham, a great deal of musical performance came my way, not only within the University Music Society but also in and around Birmingham. On a number of occasions I played as an 'extra' for the CBO, and when the second oboist had to leave to do national service, the principal oboist tried to persuade me to apply for his place. This I declined to do for several reasons. My main reason was that I was not prepared to abandon my University course before completion. In addition, I had no wish to become a full-time orchestral player, because I disliked the prospect of losing the precious element of choice in my work. Nor did I fancy full-time playing in an orchestra with some of whose members I felt ill at ease and with a conductor with whom I felt no rapport; nor would I have enjoyed some of the music which I would have been required to play.

At some point during 1947 or 1948, I was approached, at the beginning of a concert, in which I was playing with the CBO, by the principal trombone player who thrust a form into my hand and said curtly "Sign this before you leave. It's an application for membership of the Musicians' Union!" I said that I was not engaged in full-time playing, and did not wish to join the M.U. He replied that the other players could not play with me if I did not join. I refused to join, and from that time onward I had no further engagements either from the CBO or from the BBC Midland Light Orchestra.

By that time, however, I was becoming more and more involved in chamber music and solo playing. A friend of mine, Helen Barrett, who was also on the Staff of the School of Music, formed a quartet which she invited me to join. We were called the 'Clavis Quartet', and we gave some very interesting recitals at the Royal Society of Artists' Galleries in New Street, Birmingham and also out of Town.

I also played from time to time at Wolverhampton and Staffordshire Technical College in the orchestra of Dr. Percy Young's Music Department. He had an excellent small choir, and his choice of music was always interesting. A young student of the Department, Elizabeth Neve, wished to have oboe lessons, and Dr. Young invited me to teach her. A short time later, he offered me the opportunity of teaching 'Rudiments of Music' in one of the evening classes in his Department.

I began doing so on 29th September, 1947. The following year, he gave me more evening classes to teach and I gradually became quite substantially involved in the activities of the Department.

1948 was the year of Wolverhampton Centenary Pageant, for which Dr. Young was commissioned to compose all the music. He wrote a full orchestral score, and he asked me to copy from it all the individual orchestral parts. I enjoyed doing this work but it came at a time when I was preparing for my final examinations at Birmingham University, so I was far more than usually busy. I was also engaged to play in the orchestra throughout the Pageant.

Introducing . . .

THE AUTHOR

L. du GARDE PEACH,

Author, Dramatist, Lecturer, Producer; born 1890. A Yorkshireman by birth but of a Somerset family, with an ancestor who was hanged by Bloody Judge Jeffreys after Monmouth's Rebellion; also of Huguenot strain on mother's side.

Educated Manchester Grammar School and University, also Göttingen University, Germany and Sheffield University.—M.A., Ph.D.

A profound believer in peace "... but obliged twice to hold His Majesty's Commission, in two wars, owing to the stupidity of other people."

Has always been a writer, but obliged to earn a living in the academic world as a University lecturer after the 1914-18 war; took to whole-time writing in 1926; has written many stage plays, books, film scripts and about 400 radio plays; has a considerable reputation as a theatrical producer.

THE PRODUCER

T. HEATH JOYCE began his theatrical career at the age of eighteen carrying the hind-quarters of a deer across the stage for £2 a week; nine monthslater was playingthe second male lead in the same play in London. Leaving the "straight" theatre for the "musical" earned £4 a week with a revue for which he had written the material, and in which he had twenty-two changes a night, and had to look after a hundred and fifty supers who were freshly recruited in every town played. Later took over the job of producing these supers into nine scenes in the revue every Sunday evening after a train journey so that they were ready to open on Monday.

Since those days has alternated between acting, producing, and writing—sometimes with musical shows, sometimes with plays. Has written and produced for West End Revues; for five years produced, wrote and acted at Scarborough Floral Hall, and at Scarborough produced his first pageant before the war. His second after his discharge from the Royal Air Force, was at the Stoll Theatre, London, when he played the Herald-Narrator. Since then has been with the Old Vic besides being responsible for further pageants at Sheffield and Warrington.

The Music

USIC required for an occasion such as the Centenary Pageant presents certain definite problems to the composer. The librettist imposes one set of limitations, the producer another, but where close contact with these partners is achieved—as has been here—the possibility of underlining the spirit of the production with colourful, though not obtrusive, music is fascinating.

Some of the music is comic, some tragic, some imbued with a sense of pageantry; these qualities appear because they are demanded before the composer sets to work.

But there are many practical problems. The choir must be divisible into sections, each self-contained; the orchestra must be small enough to be contained within the orchestral pit, yet large enough to have much variety of colour; the solo items must be adaptable and relatively easy to memorise.

The score has involved the composition, orchestration and arrangement of some 8,000 bars of music.

The composer has in no case relied on 'period' pieces, although there are frequent passing allusions to church and folk music. The general texture is, as should be, modern, but neither aggressive nor tuneless. The overture follows precedent in outlining some of the melodies to be heard later while the initial fanfare symbolises the spirit of the Pageant. Thereafter choruses, processional music (in which effective use is made of the organ), ballet music, and many dances—among which are waltzes, polkas and even one "hot number"—follow in due order.

The final, canonic chorus declares, triumphantly, pride in the achievements of the past; bells ring out the last climax proclaiming, over the voices of the choir, faith in the future.

THE COMPOSER

PERCY M. YOUNG, M.A., Mus.D.

University Prizeman, research scholar, author and composer; is Head of the Music Department of the Wolverhampton and Staffordshire Technical College. Authoritative on the dramatic music of the Jacobean and Caroline courts he has himself written music for Yeats and Moliere productions. After leaving Cambridge he held two other important educational posts—at Belfast and Stoke-on-Trent. Since coming to the Midlands he has conducted widely, has broadcast and has toured Belgium and Holland with children's choirs. Recently he has done pioneer work on *Handel*, publishing a notable biography last year while the oratorios are the subject of a forthcoming book. Dr. Young's two memorable performances of "Messiah," as nearly as possible to *Handel's* intention, have made their mark on the musical life of the district, while his work at the College is already bearing its first fruits.

A page from the programme of Wolverhampton Centenary Pageant – June, 1948

A near-crisis arose when the dates of performances were announced: May 22nd to June 5th, 1948. These dates coincided exactly with my Finals! One of my problems was transport. I was still dependent on buses, and I spent a great deal of time travelling between Blackheath, Birmingham and Wolverhampton, returning home late at night. I used my bus journeys for doing revision for examinations, whenever possible. However, the Pageant was a great success – and I was awarded my B.A. Degree!

I celebrated my degree by going on holiday with Helen Barrett who had a particular interest in the West Country, since her mother had been born in the Lizard Lighthouse. We sketched a route for between two and three weeks' cycling, then we cleaned up our bicycles and prepared to go.

Dr. Percy M. Young

We left home on Saturday, 24th July and rode fifty-two miles, spending our first night at Gloucester. Bed and breakfast cost us nine shillings and sixpence each! Here is an extract from my diary of the tour:

'Sunday, 25th July, 1948: Left Gloucester at 9.30 a.m. and crossed the Cotswolds via Painswick and Stroud, Nailsworth ... Dunkirk, Cross Houses, then down very steeply into Bath. The climb up the Cotswolds had been long and steep, and very hot; the level stretch over the top seemed all uphill because of a strong headwind, and the descent into Bath was an anxious one owing to its steepness and excessive length, and to the consequent fact that wrist strain was great because of braking hard.

Our arrival in Bath was greeted by many disdainful looks from pious inhabitants, and as we were made to feel that we were offending the sense of propriety of the good people there, we made our exit as speedily as the gradient of the Wells Road would permit. We left Bath at 7.30 p.m., with the main objective, Wells, still 20 miles away. The crossing of the Mendips, against a headwind, at the end of a strenuous day, was no easy matter, but we plodded silently on (having no spare energy with which to be sociable), and eventually we arrived in Wells, at 11.00 p.m., very weary. After making several enquiries from the few people who were still about in the dim streets, we were able to trace the whereabouts of our lodging-place, and fortunately, the good lady there had, even at that hour, not quite despaired of our arrival, and was waiting for us. After a very welcome cup of tea, we went to bed.

Cyclometer: 60 miles. Bed and breakfast: 8/9d. each'

Three Graduates – Mary Randall, Œnone Wooldridge and Hilda Hunter, 1948

1948

We visited many places in Devon and Cornwall, and decided that we would give a recital at Land's End, the nearest church to which was Sennen. Helen was a brilliant accompanist, and organist and she had an excellent soprano voice. I had taken my oboe with me on the tour, since I could never bear to be parted from it! Here is another Diary entry:

> Sunday, 8th August, 1948. Left Buryas Bridge by the 10.00 a.m. bus to Sennen. Went straight to Tower Farm on arrival there, left our luggage, then went across to Sennen Church, and crept in to the service, which had already begun. Saw the Rector afterwards, and asked if he would like such music as we could provide, at the evening service. He gladly accepted, and allowed us to practise right away. Later, we walked down to Land's End, where we picnicked on the cliffs. We returned to Sennen for tea, after which we made our way to the Rectory, as arranged. At 6.10 p.m., the Rector took us over to the Church and escorted us to the Rectory pew. He gave us the whole of his sermon time in which to play.

> *Programme:*

> Brother James' Air (Soprano and oboe with organ)

> Loeillet: Sonata in C (oboe and organ)

> Purcell: Sound the Trumpet (soprano and oboe with organ)

> The congregation was very small, but very appreciative. Several members stayed behind and talked with us afterwards. The Rector, who knew Halesowen Church (and had known Canon Timothy Davies at Oxford), took us round the Church and Cemetery, and promised to send me a magazine. We returned to Tower Farm for supper, and found that at least two people from there had been at the evening service and had also enjoyed our music. From Tower Farm we could see Longships Light, Wolf Rock Light and the flashes from a lighthouse on the Scilly Isles.

> Supper, Bed and Breakfast: 10/6d each.

We visited the Lizard Lighthouse, Helen's target on our journey, and we were taken round by the Keeper. My diary says that he told us: 'The power of the lamp is 6,000 candle power, magnified by means of 200 prisms to 6,000,000 candle power. The whole light revolves slowly in a trough of mercury. There is only one light in the country like the Lizard light, and that is at St. Catherine's, on the Atlantic side of the Isle of Wight.' The Keeper had recently come to the Lizard from Amble, Northumberland, and knew Newbiggin-by-sea (where my cousins lived) very well..

On our homeward journey we were both smitten down by gastro-enteritis as a consequence of eating mouldy pastry and sour sausage at Redruth in Cornwall. However, after some medication and a couple of days' rest at Boscastle (where we saw a Cornish Floral Dance), we were able to resume our journey.

I had the only puncture of the tour; it happened when I was walking down Porlock Hill, which, with a laden bicycle, looked too steep to ride safely!

An interesting entry for Saturday, 14th August reminds me of an amusing overnight resting-place.

We spent last night in a house where the main decorations on the walls were illuminated texts; the only reading matter was the 'Christian Herald'; a photograph of a tombstone hung by my side of the bed and our traycloth at breakfast was a page of 'Christian Herald', some of which, including part of a biblical crossword, had been sacrificed in a brave effort to make the page fit the tray. Breakfast consisted mainly of exceedingly tough scrambled egg on toast. We spent our time and attention working as much as remained on the tray of the crossword, and it did do something to distract our thoughts from the breakfast.

We travelled on through north Devon, but by the time we reached Cheddar, Helen was very much handicapped by a strained knee. The weather was very cold and wet, and we decided to take a train from Bristol to Birmingham. We had done a tour of 25 days, and had actually cycled 508 miles.

After one of my piano lessons, I was talking with Frank Edwards about my travelling problems, and he said: "Your greatest need, now, is a motor car. You can't really afford to spend all that time travelling by bus". A statement from him to that effect was much more likely to be taken seriously by my parents than if it had been my idea alone, and I could not afford to buy a car myself at that time.

That was when Albert Mason arrived quite unexpectedly to visit Father, who had not seen him since 1918 - thirty years previously! He had built up a successful transport-business, and was surprised that we had no car. A week later, he came again, in a second-hand Austin 8 which he had found for us in Sunderland and he persuaded Father to buy it, promising that he would teach us all to drive.

Within three months I had passed my Driving Test and so had Doris; Father was still struggling and never qualified even to take the test. Though it was a family car, I had the greatest need and use of it, and I was enabled to re-arrange my activities and to use my time much more efficiently.

The number of my students at Birmingham School of Music was increasing and I also had one or two who came to my home for lessons at weekends. One, in particular, a young man who came from Rugby on Sunday mornings, was most amusing, since he sent me the occasional sketch to illustrate his oboe-generated frustration!

Sketches from a frustrated student!

When I was engaged to play in concerts I was sometimes asked if I had a competent student who could play with me. Several of my students were enabled to gain valuable experience in this way.

In 1951 I was asked by Dr. Edmunds if I could organise an evening of music with my students at the School of Music. This I was able to do. We put together and presented a varied programme which was musically effective and quite unique.

Advertisement for Concert of Music for Oboes 27th October, 1951
Photo: W. Hunter

Between 1945 and 1951 I attended several Summer Schools of Music, sometimes in the company of Birmingham University students. These schools gave brief opportunities of taking part in choral singing, which I enjoyed. I remember particularly a performance of Mozart's *Requiem Mass* conducted by Dr. Reginald Jacques, and another of Vaughan Williams' *Five Mystical Songs* which I had never previously heard.

Birmingham and Midland Institute

BIRMINGHAM SCHOOL OF MUSIC
Principal: Christopher Edmunds, D.Mus.,F.T.C.L.,F.B.S.M.,

C O N C E R T   O F   M U S I C   F O R   O B O E S

by students of HILDA HUNTER, B.A.,L.R.A.M.

on SATURDAY, 27th OCTOBER, 1951, at 7:0 p.m.

in the SMALL THEATRE
(Doors open at 6:30 o'clock).

OBOES:

Maurice Abbott   Dr.D.R.Humphreys
  (and Cor Anglais)   Mollie Jackson
Magdalen Andrews   Herbert Jurevics
Noreen Brailsford   Elizabeth Neve
William E. Bury   Barry Priddey
Professor Brodie Hughes   Barbara Wilmot

VIOLONCELLO: Christine Baugh

ACCOMPANISTS: Dr. Ruth Gipps
               Mollie Jackson
               Susan Neve

- - - - - - - - -

<u>Programme overleaf</u>

P R O G R A M M E

OVERTURE - Esther   G. F. Handel
                                       Ensemble

CONCERTO - First Movement   Rutland Boughton
                                   Maurice Abbott

ELEGY on the death of Queen Mary Henry Purcell
                               Magdalen Andrews &
                                   Barbara Wilmot

PIECE   Cesar Franck
                                   Elizabeth Neve

CONCERTO in D minor, Op.20 - First Movement
                                      Ruth Gipps
                                   Barry Priddey
      (accompanied by the composer)

TWO CANZONETS   Thomas Morley
            Maurice Abbott & Noreen Brailsford.

TRIO SONATA in F major - two movements
                                   J.B. Loeillet
            Magdalen Andrews & Barbara Wilmot

CONCERTO - First Movement   Richard Strauss
                                 Herbert Jurevics

SONATA from Church Cantata, No. 31 -
    "Der Himmel Lacht, die Erde jubilieret"
                                      J.S.Bach
                                      Ensemble

I have a vivid memory of the singing of one student on the St. Andrews Course of 1949. I think her name was Grace and she came from Perth. She had a clear, even-toned soprano voice of magnificent and unaffected quality, and she controlled it with ease and assurance. She sang 'Ihr habt nun Traurigkeit' from Brahms's *Requiem* with amazing maturity of understanding yet with purity and simplicity of sound. I remember feeling overwhelmed by the sincerity and beauty of her singing.

The summer schools also presented opportunities of hearing performances by eminent people and of attending concentrated courses of lectures given by eminent teachers. One unforgettable performance took place at Downe House, Newbury, in 1951, when Arthur Cranmer, who had lectured on singing, joined forces with his son, Philip, who had lectured on the art of accompaniment, to give a recital of quite outstanding musical quality. Their lectures had been delightful, as both had a very keen sense of humour as well as outstanding musicianship. I recall a demonstration by Philip of how some accompanists literally 'follow the soloist' instead of their being exactly together. He sang 'The Vagabond' by Vaughan Williams, whilst playing his own accompaniment very slightly late throughout the song – a most difficult feat for an accompanist accustomed to precision and to the highest standards of musicianship in all his performances!

Summer Music School at Coleg Harlech – 1947
Dr. Percy Young, Dr. Thomas Armstrong and Students of Birmingham University
(H.H. is second left)

Photo: Eric Merriman

Summer Music School at Downe House, Newbury – 1951

Arthur and Philip Cranmer

Photo: Hilda Hunter

For some time I had been aware that my oboe playing depended on my one and only instrument. (I had sold my little four-guineas oboe back to Yardley's in Birmingham, from whom I originally bought it, for the same price as I had paid for it!) The firm of T. W. Howarth had recently started to make oboes, and when I took my Louis oboe to them for a 'check-up', I tried one of the new instruments and fell in love with its sound and its handling qualities. I ordered one then and there, and I went to London again to collect it shortly afterwards, on 18th October, 1948. It was their fifteenth instrument, Number 1015, and it cost £144. 4s. 6d. It has given me wonderful service and endless enjoyment in playing, and when I took it to Howarth's for a check-up after nearly fifty years of its busy life, it was found to be perfect! Several of my students subsequently bought Howarth oboes and derived great pleasure from playing them.

An event of historical importance in the musical life of Wolverhampton took place on 15th March, 1950. This was the occasion when the opera *Riders to the Sea*, by Ralph Vaughan Williams, was performed in the presence of the composer, at Wolverhampton and Staffordshire Technical College by members of the College Singers and Orchestra. The soloists in particular, who were all members of the Music Department, gave performances of outstanding musical quality and beauty. The entire event was due to the initiative of Dr. Percy Young, who trained singers and orchestra and directed the performance. Dr. Vaughan Williams was most impressed and very complimentary.

Dr. Young's services to music have been honoured in many ways and in many places. His most recent accolade has been his election, in 1998, to an Honorary Life Fellowship of Selwyn College, Cambridge.

For some time I had felt that, instead of depending on an accumulation of part-time work, I ought to look for a full-time post in order to stabilise my future finances. During 1952 some reorganisation of courses at Wolverhampton and Staffordshire Technical College resulted in students of practical skills, such as engineering, plumbing or building, being required to study a cultural subject for one hour weekly. Music was a popular choice, so more work in the Music Department became available, and Dr. Young took the opportunity of creating for me a full-time post as Assistant Lecturer in Music. This was a welcome appointment. I resigned from Birmingham School of Music, and some other part-time commitments and concentrated on Wolverhampton.

Dr. Young is one of a small number of people for whose encouragement I shall always be grateful. He helped me in many ways, one of which was to ask me to do what I believed impossible and then to prove me wrong! An instance of this was his request that I compose a short work for oboe and strings for performance at a forthcoming concert. Composition did not come easily to me and I judged myself incapable of this. He judged otherwise and I wrote a short quintet movement which we played in the Civic Hall, Wolverhampton, some time in the early 50's.

I had been drawing the musical illustrations for a series of books called 'The Student's Music Library' which Dr. Young edited for the publisher Dennis Dobson. These illustrations had to be drawn with great care in 'jumbo-size' manuscript, from which they were photographically reduced and reproduced by the publisher. On returning from one of his visits to see Dennis Dobson, Dr. Young said to me: "I have promised that you will write a book, and the publisher needs it by 1st October. It will be called *The Grammar of Music!*" I said "I can't do *that*!" Dr. Young believed otherwise, gave me some guidance on preparation, and the book was ready on time and published in 1952.

I was also teaching recorder playing in Dr. Young's Music Department, and he encouraged me to put on performances by the oboe and recorder students, which I did from time to time. There is nothing like the prospect of a performance to improve the playing of students, and my groups gained valuable experience from these opportunities of using their skills.

In early 1953 I was invited by Dr. Walter Bergmann to play oboe in a concert at the Central Hall, Birmingham, and to take with me a competent pupil. I took Neil Black along and we both enjoyed the experience of playing chamber music with recorders, strings and continuo. Subsequently, Dr. Bergmann invited us to play for him in London. Shortly afterwards, Neil moved permanently to London, and played for Dr. Bergmann on a number of occasions.

Dr. Bergmann was one of a number of eminent musicians who had left Germany in the early 1930's and who had been interned in England for the duration of the war. My parents enjoyed his company and he became a family friend. He was a most industrious musician. As well as being a composer, conductor and musicologist, he made a vast repertoire of music available to recorder players by making sensitive arrangements of well-known and lesser-known music, thereby ensuring the continuing life of the recorder movement. Sadly, he died, on 13th January, 1988.

I had had a long association with Aberystwyth which, for many years, had been a favourite place for family holidays. During one such holiday I was taken to Siloh Chapel (unfortunately now demolished) to hear a recital by Charles Clements, playing organ, and Mary Jarred who sang contralto solos. This must have been during my schooldays. The performance impressed me enormously. I have no recollection of the programme, but the playing and singing were wonderful.

I had known Dr. Ian Parrott as a Music Lecturer at Birmingham University, and after his appointment as Professor of Music at the University College of Wales, Aberystwyth, he invited me from time to time to play in his orchestral concerts there. I always enjoyed those visits and I made some good friends among the musicians with whom I played.

Professor Parrott and Dr. Bergmann shared the conducting of a concert which concluded a Weekend of Recorder Playing at Gregynog Hall in June, 1955. The participants came from London, the Midlands and Aberystwyth.

When, in 1955, I was invited by Professor Parrott to join the Staff of his Department, I was delighted. In many ways I was sorry to leave Wolverhampton because of the friends I would leave behind, but I succumbed to the temptation of making music in the fresh air of Wales!

Gregynog Hall

(*Photos: Theo Wyatt*)

Miss Davies of Gregynog (front row, third from right) with the assembled musicians
(H.H. is front row, fourth from right)

Photo: *Theo Wyatt*

PROGRAMME

OF A

CONCERT OF MUSIC FOR VOICES,
RECORDERS, OBOES AND STRINGS

AT

GREGYNOG

ON

SATURDAY, JUNE 4th, 1955

AT 3 P.M.

MARY RANDALL		Soprano
MARGARET WALTON		Contralto
ARTHUR DAWES		Bass

THE GREGYNOG CHOIR

Recorders
Walter Bergmann . Theo Wyatt . Elli McMullen
Hilda Hunter

Oboes
Hilda Hunter . Barbara Wilmot . Professor Brodie Hughes

Cor Anglais
Barbara Wilmot

Strings
(violins)
Edward Bor . Edith O'Hanrahan . Enid Parry

(viola)
Raymond Jeremy

(violoncello)
John Clapham

Harpsichord
Walter Bergmann

Conductors
Walter Bergmann *and* Professor Ian Parrott

PROGRAMME

1. Concerto for four treble recorders,
   strings and continuo   *J. D. Heinichen*

2. "The Morning"
   Cantata for soprano voice, sopranino
   recorder, strings and continuo   *T. A. Arne*

3. Concerto Grosso in A minor
   for two treble recorders, strings
   and continuo   *G. P. Telemann*

4. Concerto Grosso in B flat
   for two treble recorders,
   two oboes, strings and continuo *G.P.Telemann*

5. "Komm, du susse Todestunde"
   aria (from Cantata 161) for contralto voice,
   treble and tenor recorders
   and continuo   *J. S. Bach*

6. Cantata 140: "Sleepers, Wake!"
   for soprano and bass soloists, chorus,
   oboes, strings and continuo   *J. S. Bach*

INTERVAL

Recorder Weekend at Gregynog – some of the musicians
Hilda Hunter, Dr. Walter Bergmann, Mary Randall, Professor Brodie Hughes
and Barbara Wilmot

Professor Ian Parrott, Mary Randall, Professor Brodie Hughes and Barbara Wilmot
Phoro: H. Hunter

Chapter 8:

MIGRATION, MID-WALES AND MASTERY

Radio Times (Incorporating World-Radio)   August 5, 1955.
Vol. 128 : No. 1656.   Registered at the G.P.O. as a Newspaper
WELSH EDITION

BBC SOUND AND TELEVISION
PROGRAMMES . . . AUGUST 7—13

RADIO TIMES

JOURNAL OF THE BBC

PRICE THREEPENCE

THE VISIT TO WALES OF
Her Majesty the Queen
On Monday Her Majesty the Queen and His Royal
Highness the Duke of Edinburgh visit Aberystwyth
where Her Majesty opens the completed building of
the National Library of Wales: Home and Television
Details of broadcasts covering the Royal visit are given on page 3

My appointment at the University College of Wales, Aberystwyth, was as 'Teacher of Piano and Woodwind, and Librarian of the Music Department', and my first task was to revitalise the Music Library. It had suffered a long period of neglect, resulting in a generous overlay of cobwebs on books and furniture, and there was no catalogue. I worked on the Library for a month, prior to the beginning of the 1955-6 Session, alternating dustpan and brush with the establishment of an index system and the start of a catalogue.

On 8th August, 1955, Aberystwyth was honoured by a Royal visit. Her Majesty Queen Elizabeth II and H.R.H. The Duke of Edinburgh came, and the Queen opened the Gregynog Wing of the National Library of Wales. This new wing completed the building of the National Library. The Queen also opened the new Headquarters of the Welsh Plant Breeding Station of the University of Wales, at Plas Gogerddan just on the edge of the town. There was great anticipation and preparation, and huge excitement when the day arrived. During the proceedings at the National Library, the Aberystwyth Madrigal Singers and a small orchestra played a programme of music. The conductors were Professor Ian Parrott and Charles Clements, and I was privileged to play oboe in the small orchestra.

Her Majesty Queen Elizabeth II opening the Gregynog Wing of the National Library of Wales, Aberystwyth, 8th August, 1955
Photograph by courtesy of Mr. Glynn Pickford

Charles Clements was a great favourite in the Music Department. He was a man of long and honourable experience who had been the friend of many an eminent musician – a legend throughout Wales. He was quiet and unassuming, disliking publicity of any kind. As a pianist, organist and especially as an accompanist, he was second to none, and as a conductor of singers and instrumentalists he had the gift of drawing the best from his performers by encouragement, kind firmness, and not a little wit. His musical integrity was total and he did not suffer fools gladly. Those of us who were privileged to play solo to his accompaniment experienced a very special partnership of musical thought and feeling. Students and Staff loved and respected him, and to work with him was sheer joy.

Every Monday at 5.30 p.m. there was a concert in the Examination Hall of the University. This series of concerts was always well attended, both by University Students and Staff, and by a very faithful gathering of members of the general public. Performances were organised by Edward Bor, the leader of the College Quartet, who frequently invited me to take part. These chamber music events were very enjoyable to rehearse, as well as to present; there was a great warmth between audience and performers.

The College Orchestra and Choir also met regularly and periodically presented concerts, usually conducted by the Professor. On one occasion, *The Dark Night of the Soul* by Edmund Rubbra was played, in the presence of the composer. The students had their own Choir and Orchestra, conducted by a student; they invited members of Music Department Staff to play in their concerts.

From time to time, performances were given outside the College. For many years, the Misses Davies had invited and given hospitality to the most eminent and internationally famous musicians, at Gregynog, their wonderful home in the country. We felt ourselves very privileged also to be invited from time to time, and we gave a number of concerts there. These visits were always most enjoyable and we were made very welcome.

In the Music Department, a great deal of instrumental teaching went on, alongside the academic work. Edward Bor was responsible for string teaching and I was responsible for woodwind. By that time, I had not only my oboe, oboe d'amore (used mainly in works by J. S. Bach), and cor anglais, but I also possessed and had learned to play bassoon, flute and clarinet. The bassoon was my particular favourite, since it allowed me to play in the bass range of the orchestra.

I had quite a number of piano students, who were a joy to teach since they had already acquired good musical experience. I had no paper qualification in piano teaching, though in Wolverhampton I had had several fairly advanced students, two of whom gained L.R.A.M. diplomas whilst they studied with me. In one of my vacations at Aberystwyth, therefore, I worked for and obtained an A.R.C.M. diploma in Piano Teaching. In a later vacation, I decided to update my oboe qualification and obtained an F.T.C.L. Oboe Performer's Diploma.

University College of Wales, Aberystwyth
Staff and Students of Music Department 1955-56
(H.H. is front row, fourth from right)

During my first year in Aberystwyth, I was privileged to have rooms in the home of Sir Idris and Lady Bell. Though they were not musicians, they were both intensely loyal to the Music Department and attended all the concerts. They were very kind to me, and invited me to join them on many occasions when they were entertaining family, or friends from the town or from further afield. Lady Bell's Sunday Tea Parties were legendary; they were events to which members of College Staff were invited, and I met people from other Departments whom I might not otherwise have known.

When Sir Idris knew that I was arranging to go on holiday with Lucy Vincent to Milan, Rome and Florence in July, 1956, he took a great deal of interest, and he taught me some basic Italian, to help on our travels. He encouraged me to learn Welsh and helped me by listening to my reading of a Welsh novel, and explaining grammatical points as we went along. He was delighted when I was invited to take part in a conversation in Welsh with Mrs. Enid Parry on Welsh Radio, in her programme called 'Dyddiadur Cerdd' ('Music Diary').

Sir Harold Idris Bell and Lady Bell – 1956

Photo: H. Hunter

Unfortunately, I had only one year of residence with the Bells, though I was a frequent visitor during the whole of my stay in Aberystwyth. At the end of my first year, I was invited by the College to become Sub-Warden of Alexandra Hall of Residence for Women Students. There, I was in charge of the Annexe for a year. It was a very dull house and I did not enjoy my accommodation in a large back room, after having become used to the light airiness of 'Bro Gynin', the Bells' house, though I enjoyed being with the students.

The other Sub-Warden of Alexandra Hall, Dr. Alice Evans, was a very good friend to me. She taught me to ride, and we went out together on hired ponies in the Dyfi Valley. She told me that she had realised on the first occasion of my visiting Alexandra Hall that I was 'one of us' when I described having taken Mother in the car over the byways high up in Plynlimon one New Year's Day!

I was invited in the following year to be Warden of Ceredigion Hall, where I had first floor rooms overlooking the sea, which gave me a much more pleasant outlook. There were seventy students to care for, and I was ably helped by Alice Jones, my Domestic Bursar, who was very competent and most faithful and loyal to me. Lucy Vincent came to stay with me on one occasion. I was able to take her up into the mountains which she loved, as I did, and she was very happy.

Lucy Vincent at Harlech, 1958

Photo: H. Hunter

I was able to go home fairly often, and from time to time I brought Mother and Mary back with me to spend a holiday at their favourite seaside resort. They, too, loved being taken up in the hills, where there were some wonderfully remote places from which one had glorious views. They were always made very welcome by the Bells, whom they visited many times.

The County Music Organiser of Montgomeryshire, Peter Davies, approached Edward Bor and asked if he and I would be prepared to go to Newtown on some Saturdays to teach pupils from County schools who had been specially selected, mainly on the evidence of their recorder playing, for their apparent musical potential. We agreed to do so. Edward taught violin pupils and I was invited to teach oboe and bassoon. Instruments were provided by the County and were loaned to pupils, who were subsequently encouraged to buy their own.

These pupils were drawn from all parts of Montgomeryshire, a rural county with widely scattered communities, and many had very long journeys to make to reach Newtown for their lessons. They were most enthusiastic and very keen to learn, and without exception they were a delight to teach. I had a bassoon pupil who was said to be somewhat troublesome in his school. He worked hard and made excellent progress on his instrument, soon becoming able to demonstrate his prowess by playing solos and gaining a good Grade VIII certificate from the Associated Board of the Royal Schools of Music. I was told that his school work and behaviour improved out of all recognition!

Montgomeryshire young musicians in Newtown – 1964
A break in lessons –
"We have to go and play at the Proclamation of the Eisteddfod – back soon!"
Photo: Hilda Hunter

I had an oboe pupil whose father brought him to his first lesson, and, with some diffidence, asked me afterwards if I thought that David would make a good oboist. I replied that he had made more progress in his first lesson than any pupil I had previously taught – with one exception – and that I thought his potential as an oboist was excellent. He was barely eleven years old at the time. At the age of twenty-four, he became Principal Oboe in the BBC Symphony Orchestra! He leads a full life as an orchestral, chamber music and solo player and a teacher. He has travelled widely and gained great experience. David Theodore has established for himself an international reputation and is now widely regarded as an authority on oboe playing and teaching.

David Theodore c. 1959
Photo: H. Hunter

David Theodore outside the Chiltern Street Showrooms of
T.W. Howarth and Co. Ltd., London – 1997
Photo: Peter Beaumont

The Montgomeryshire children were given many opportunities of orchestral playing. There was a County Youth Orchestra which met for weekend and full week courses, and the Mid-Wales Youth Orchestra included Montgomeryshire, together with Cardiganshire, Brecon and Radnor when it held courses and gave concerts annually, in each county in succession. The best players auditioned for the National Youth Orchestra of Wales, or for the British National Youth Orchestra, and, after that experience, a number of players gained professional appointments.

The Mid-Wales Youth Orchestra with Rae Jenkins (guest Conductor), Peter Davies (Music Organiser, Montgomeryshire and Conductor), and Tutorial Staff, c. 1960 (H.H. is second row, third from right)

Peter Davies was an excellent and very hardworking County Music Organiser. He knew every one of the instrumental pupils – and also the members of the Youth Choir, for which he was responsible – and was aware of their school and family backgrounds. He was also very good to his Staff, and he had their loyalty in full measure. He organised a variety of music courses, and engaged appropriate staff members as coaches of their particular instruments. He built up musical activity among the young people of the County to a very high level indeed, by his unstinting devotion of time and energy to their needs and by the generous use of his own personal musical skills. Music-making in Montgomeryshire was a very happy and stimulating experience for all of us – pupils and tutors alike.

Another of my musical involvements began in 1957 when I was invited to attend the Music Teachers' Association Summer School of Music at Matlock, to assist Dr. Walter Bergmann in Recorder teaching.

The Matlock Courses were held in the Training College and were designed to provide instruction in practical music-making in schools. They were attended mainly by young teachers. The members of Staff were drawn from teachers of very wide experience and one gained a great deal from conversation with them. The atmosphere at these courses was always extremely happy, due in no small part to the efficiency of the Secretary of the M.T.A., Mrs. Eileen Craine, who ensured the smooth working of a complex organisation with minimum of fuss and maximum goodwill and apparent light-heartedness.

After some years of our partnership, Dr. Bergmann became involved in musical activities abroad which clashed with the dates of the Matlock courses, and I was given responsibility for all recorder work. Sometime later, the courses were transferred to York University, where they continued very happily for several years more, until expenses became too great for their continuance. The last course took place in 1975.

During those courses, members of Staff were sometimes requested by the M.T.A. to give private lessons to students. One such student came to me for oboe lessons. She was an interesting but intensely shy and diffident young school teacher – Marie Isherwood, later Mrs. Marie Tomlinson – from Clitheroe in Lancashire. We had some long lessons during which she told me a great deal about her musical activities in the primary school in which she taught. I liked her personality and admired the way in which she regarded her musical commitment. I told her that she had a great deal to offer and that her musical potential was far greater than she realised. I suggested – with a sensation of *déjà vue*, since this is what Lucy had advised me, many years before – that she should seek to become less self-effacing and acknowledge, and exploit to the full, her obvious musical talent. She eventually became a County Music Adviser for Lancashire Education Authority, and she subsequently had an additional rôle as overall General Adviser to a group of Primary Schools. More recently, she became an Ofsted Inspector!

Professor Brodie Hughes had, over the years, gradually changed his rôle from being my oboe student to becoming my mentor. He visited me at Aberystwyth, and could see, at least as clearly as I could and possibly more so, that I was heading towards another 'cul-de-sac' in my professional activities. He diagnosed a 'deficiency of academic stimulation' and advised me to embark on work for a higher degree, suggesting research into relation-ships between music and various states of mental health. He offered me facilities in his department to carry out research.

I was told that there were Regulations for the Degree of M.A. for Full-time Members of Staff in the University of Wales, and I obtained the necessary permission to register for this degree. In subsequent vacations I did my research in Birmingham, and by 1960 I had my thesis prepared.

Other events were taking place concurrently. At The Royal Normal College for the Blind, Rowton Castle, Shrewsbury, a vacancy had arisen for someone to take over the Music Department, and Doris, who had for some years been Head of the Typing Department, urged me to apply for the post. Music and Typing were the two components of the training of senior girls at Rowton Castle; senior boys were sited at Albrighton Hall, Shrewsbury, and I was led to understand that they were a separate entity. My parents were advancing in age and it seemed an attractive proposition to move nearer to home – fifty miles away instead of one hundred and twenty.

The post at Rowton Castle appeared to present a challenge and to have sufficient scope for my musical energies. It was offered to me, together with a promise of the provision of instruments for the students, and the opportunity for me to continue with my teaching in Montgomeryshire on Saturdays, and my playing in concerts as far as these were compatible with my daily work. I accepted the post and left Aberystwyth at the end of 1960. Very soon afterwards, several other musicians left, too.

My final performance at Aberystwyth was a lecture-recital on woodwind instruments, in which I was accompanied by Charles Clements. Just prior to the recital, I was preparing my array of instruments which I intended to assemble in view of the audience as the lecture progressed. I could not find my little sopranino recorder, and having searched among my collection I still failed to locate it. I dashed back to Charlie's house where we had been rehearsing, but no recorder there. Back to the University Examination Hall to begin my lecture without it.

I described and played my bamboo pipe, then made my apologies for the absence of its counterpart, the sopranino recorder. I talked about the family of recorders, descant, treble, tenor, bass, and about the contra-bass which Dr. Bergmann had very kindly lent me for the occasion. I discussed their sizes in relation to each other, explained something of their acoustical properties and differing tone qualities, and played music on each in turn.

Similarly, I assembled, talked about and played my flute, oboe, oboe d'amore, cor anglais and clarinets in B flat and A, explaining about the 'transposing instruments' as I introduced them. Then I came to the bassoon, and began to assemble it, fitting the bass-joint and the wing into the double-joint. Then, as I took the bell out of my bassoon case, I saw the tell-tale loop of pink ribbon emerging from its end. I pulled the ribbon and out came the red woolly sock containing my errant sopranino recorder! The audience thought this hilarious and would not believe that it was not deliberately planned! I proceeded to play my belated illustration on the eight-inch long sopranino, and made an ultra-effective comparison between that and the eight-foot long bassoon, on which I played my final music. Charlie and I enjoyed our evening; the audience were happy, too!

Doris was exceedingly amiable at this time, and she had offered to type my M.A. thesis. Towards the end of 1960, she came to Aberystwyth for a few days, and my thesis was typed and checked with the utmost care and precision. Doris took a justifiable pride in her typing, and she had a complete understanding of all matters regarding layout. Nothing was too much trouble. The work went to the binders, and the final presentation was sheer perfection.

We left Ceredigion Hall together. Doris and I had been working together as she typed and she had also seen something of my life, albeit in a vacation, as Warden of a Hall of Residence, to whom a certain deference is shown. As we left, she said: "It won't be like this when you get to Rowton!" In a flash, I saw disaster lying in wait to trap me.

To make a mistake once is perhaps understandable; I should have known better than go to work at Stewarts and Lloyds, where Doris had experience and authority. But to make the same mistake a second time was sheer stupidity. I had been warned by Peter Davies that I was making a wrong decision. Foolishly, I had not heeded his advice. He was to be proved absolutely right in his prognosis of trouble ahead.

Chapter 9:

RESIGNATION AND REDIRECTION

After the Christmas holiday, in the New Year of 1961, Doris set off for the Royal Normal College for the Blind at Rowton Castle, near Shrewsbury. I followed in my own car. Doris had suggested that I give up my car and share hers, but I refused even to consider the idea. On arrival, we attended a formal afternoon tea, and I was introduced to other members of Staff. I was then shown my quarters – one room, with minimal furnishings.

Term began, students returned, and teaching commenced. My individual students were pleasant and we got on well together. I did not enjoy teaching classes of junior boys and girls, whose attitude was that music was simply another recreation period. The girls expected to be allowed to knit during 'Music Appreciation' classes and the boys came equipped with small radios and earpieces, expecting to listen to sport. When I spoke of these attitudes to the Principal, his comment was: "Well, I know nothing about music and I enjoy it, so why can't they enjoy it on the same terms?"! I retorted that I had clearly been engaged under false pretences, and that I had believed that I was appointed actually to *teach* music. However, I successfully prohibited the intrusions and worked hard to change attitudes.

A happy innovation was the formation of a madrigal group to which I invited girls who were interested. I had about twelve keen volunteers and we had weekly practices. No Braille music was available so I had to teach entirely by rote, a procedure which is non-educational, but which gave the girls an experience which would otherwise have been denied them. I reminded the Principal of his promise to provide clarinets and recorders for the use of students; I was met with a firm refusal because of a cash shortage!

I had been told that 'duty days' happened about once in ten days; in the event, they happened about twice weekly, and involved much ringing of bells, and locking or unlocking of doors at specific times, checking that students were in – or out of – their beds and supervising meals. Doris was a devoted 'duty' person, and when I said that, in my view, much of this was antiquated and useless, she took the side of the Establishment – naturally – and said that it was I who failed to understand the absolute necessity for this ritual. She was right.

The fact that I was supposed to be in charge of music at Rowton Castle turned out to be a myth, when a man from the Staff of Albrighton Hall (where senior boys lived and were taught music and piano-tuning) came to Rowton. I happened to meet him, and was told that he was 'Head of Music'. On enquiry, I discovered that he was actually in charge of music at both sites! Every new experience at Rowton was an utter disappointment and I felt let down and deceived, yet I knew that I was to blame for having allowed myself to be so misled. The situation was saved only by the senior girls, who were friendly and appreciative. I prepared a number of them for examinations of the Associated Board of the Royal Schools of Music, which they all passed, to their great delight.

My own playing suffered at this time. An oboist has to practise daily, otherwise lip-muscles get slack and uncontrollable. I could not play in my room as I would have been disturbing other members of Staff and especially Doris who was hostile to my music anyway. The few practice-rooms were fully used by students. My only way of doing oboe practice was to drive out and find a remote spot in the country.

I had one or two concert engagements already booked, and on these occasions I sensed resentment around me. The same happened when, on Saturdays, about once in three weeks, I went to Newtown to teach the Montgomeryshire students. I also visited my parents at home whenever possible, and they were in no doubt about my state of disappointment and depression.

After some weeks I fell ill with so-called influenza. For three whole weeks I had an unremitting high temperature, and I was simply told to take hot drinks and aspirin. What I could not tell anybody was that I felt totally isolated and miserable, and I had little will to recover and resume my work. I felt in total accord with the Welsh poet, John Ceiriog Hughes (1832-87), who, when 'exiled' to work as a Railway Stationmaster in Manchester, wrote the following poem, in which he expressed a longing to be home in Wales.

Nant y Mynydd

Nant y Mynydd groyw loyw,
Yn ymdroelli tua'r pant,
Rhwng y brwyn yn sisial ganu, –
O na bawn i fel y nant!

Grug y Mynydd yn eu blodau,
Edrych arnynt hiraeth ddug
Am gael aros ar y bryniau
Yn yr awel efo'r grug.

Adar mân y mynydd uchel
Godant yn yr awel iach,
O'r naill drum i'r llall yn 'hedeg, –
O na bawn fel 'deryn bach!

Mab y Mynydd ydwyf innau
Oddi cartref yn gwneud cân,
Ond mae 'nghalon yn y mynydd
Efo'r grug a'r adar mân.

Ceiriog

Mountain Stream

The clear shining mountain stream meanders towards the valley, whispering among the reeds. Would that I were like the stream!

I look at the flowering mountain heather, and I feel an angry longing to be free to stay in the hills, among the heather and in the breeze.

Little mountain birds, rising on the fresh breeze, flying from one ridge to another – would that I were like a little bird!

I, too, belong to the mountain. I am far from home, singing my song; but my heart is in the mountain with the heather and the little birds.

Easter came, and Doris had a fancy for going pony-trekking in Brecon. She had never ridden, but felt that, in the hour promised for tuition, she could learn to do so. We went together on the first trek, but, after that, Doris preferred to explore the area in her new car. I went out on all the treks over the mountains and enjoyed the fresh air and exercise. I had taken a book to read at night. It was Monica Baldwin's *I Leap over the Wall*. Suddenly, as I read, I knew I must do the same. On my return, I presented my notice of resignation to the Principal who refused to accept it, but I insisted. He renewed promises of instruments, but I said that it was all too late and that nothing he could say would affect my decision to leave.

The summer term dragged on, with just a few bright spots to relieve it. At the end of April, I heard that I had been awarded an M.A. Degree of the University of Wales. The degree ceremony was in July, before the term ended, and I was grudgingly allowed to go to Cardiff to attend it. I took Mother with me and she enjoyed her visit enormously. I brought her back over the Brecon Beacons. With my prospect of imminent freedom I felt renewed and happy, and Mother was happy that I was returning home. Doris, on the other hand, was morose during that term, and our communication with each other was minimal.

Speech Day came; my clarinet pupil played a solo and the Madrigal Group sang several madrigals quite beautifully. They gave me a china horse as a farewell gift, and were touchingly sad when I departed.

In August, the Matlock Summer School took place again and I was absorbed in music teaching and playing. On my return home I needed to think about my work in the forthcoming term. I had my Montgomeryshire teaching to look forward to, and I had to think of how to add to that whilst seeking full-time work.

I enquired of the County Music Organiser for Worcestershire whether there was any woodwind teaching needed in the County; similarly, I approached the Organiser for Shropshire. Both offered me teaching, and I began working for both in September, 1961.

During the following eighteen months I found myself driving to schools in Oldbury (Worcestershire), Bromsgrove, Kidderminster, Stourbridge, Bridgnorth, Coalbrookdale, Ludlow and Shrewsbury during weekdays, and Newtown, Montgomeryshire on Saturdays, and teaching all the woodwind orchestral instruments, some at one school and some at another. Also, I was invited by my old friends in the Midlands to play either oboe or bassoon professionally in their concerts.

This teaching was interesting in that I became aware of the differences between County Education Authorities in the importance that each attached to its peripatetic Staff, and also of the huge differences in attitude towards music between Head Teachers. For instance, in one secondary school, set among the smelly chemical works of Oldbury, there was a dedicated Headmistress whose love of music shone out through her pupils – all from indifferent backgrounds – whose good manners and enthusiasm for music and those who taught it were heart-warming.

On the other hand, on arrival at certain schools of high repute, I was expected to teach in the most abysmal accommodation imaginable. At one High School I was allocated a small turret with no windows, ventilation or heating and poor artificial light. There was a chair and a music-stand, but no table on which to unpack my instruments and teach pupils to care for theirs.

I declined to teach there and was transferred to the Sick Room, where there was sometimes competition for space! In another school I was expected to teach in the dusty, dark, low-ceilinged area beneath the school Assembly Hall stage! My refusal to do so was greeted with some surprise, so I asked the member of staff concerned whether he himself would relish being required to breathe deeply, as my students were, in such an atmosphere. Alternative accommodation was soon found!

I arrived at a Shropshire school at the appointed time and was taken by a scruffy little boy across a field to a disused barn. It had one small window, outside and close to which was an enormous tree in full leaf. The one light-socket had no bulb. There was no furniture whatever and the place was thick with dust and cobwebs. I reported the situation to the County Music Organiser, saying that I would not teach in that school unless appropriate conditions were provided. I had no reply and I never went back there.

One night, I began an attack of influenza. I could not possibly attend my Shropshire schools the following morning and I tried to telephone the Music Organiser. I could get no reply, either at her home or her office, so I telephoned each school to inform them that I could not attend. Two days later, I received a curt letter from her, saying that, in future, if I were unable to attend schools, I must telephone her directly, and not the schools concerned, and that I must always give twenty-four hours' notice of inability to attend! I was not prepared to spend a day driving a round trip of one-hundred-plus miles in all weathers (and the winter of 1962-3 was exceptionally difficult), in order to teach, and then to be treated in that way. She received my notice by return of post!

Montgomeryshire teaching continued to be a pleasure, due to Peter Davies's excellent organisation. Though my journey to Newtown on Saturdays was seventy-two miles each way, the effort was well worthwhile because of the quality of the response.

In the Spring of 1963, I applied for the post of Lecturer in Music at Wolverhampton Teachers' College for Day Students, a Constituent College of Birmingham University School of Education. On arrival for interview, I discovered that the Head of Department was none other than William Stevens Ingley whose signature had alternated with mine in the Practice Book on the organ of Halesowen Parish Church during World War II! We had both been students of Frank Edwards, and of Birmingham University Music Department, without ever having met. The other full-time Music Lecturer was Victor Garrison, whom I also knew as a violinist and as another former student of Birmingham University Music Department.

I was in London, having played in a concert for Dr. Bergmann, when the Principal of the College telephoned to offer me the post, which I readily accepted. This proved to be the beginning of fifteen very happy years of teaching in the Music Department of the College. Bill Ingley was a first-class musician and an excellent administrator. He had exceptional rapport with Staff and students, a keen wit, an interest in words and their use, and he and I were equally fastidious about detail and accuracy in all matters. There was a sizeable part-time staff of instrumental teachers – all local people and friends of ours – and we were able to give interesting and varied concerts. The annual Carol Service, held in a local Church, was always a highlight of the year. Both the College Choir and Small Choir comprised Staff and Students, and they gave some lovely performances.

The students were adults, most of whom had experience in commerce, and had a genuine keenness to become teachers. Some had families, but were now free to return to full-time education. Their enthusiasm, together with that of the Principal and his carefully selected Staff, gave the College a very special ambience which, despite its antiquated buildings in Walsall Street, made working there an experience of rare quality and pleasure.

I continued to teach woodwind in Montgomeryshire on Saturdays. In the Spring term of 1964, Peter Davies invited me to go as Woodwind Tutor, with the County Youth Orchestra and the County Girls' Choir, on a concert tour of Baden-Württemberg in West Germany, during the Easter vacation of 1964.

There were great preparations in the County and my pupil, David, was chosen to play solos in the proposed programme. I went to as many of the preparatory rehearsals as possible, and I made efforts to learn some basic German from television programmes and from Bill, who visited friends in Germany, and studied the language diligently.

I kept a diary of the tour; it includes these comments:

Saturday, 4th April: Rehearsal in morning for concert that evening. The mayor was getting anxious as the rehearsal went on (this was the only full rehearsal of the tour, and had to be reasonably thorough, though it was, in fact, not very long) and he went to Mr. Davies and said: "The history of Crailsheim awaits you . . ." meaning that plans for a brief lecture to us on the history of the town were made and the start was already overdue! After lunch we all went to 'Schloss Langenburg', the home of Princess Marguerite, sister of the Duke of Edinburgh. She showed us over the castle personally, and when she explained that the courtyard was reputed to be acoustically excellent, the choir sang some songs there and proved it so. The castle was 'in splints' and was being rebuilt, following a fire two years previously. Evening concert – lovely hall – wonderfully enthusiastic reception.

Montgomeryshire Youth Choir, conducted by Peter Davies, proving the acoustics of Schloss Langenburg in April, 1964

Saturday, 11th April: Left Kehl for Bad Godesberg. Journey along Rhine, with lunch at Hotel Traube at Rüdesheim. Wonderful scenery. On to Y.H. at Bad Godesberg. Warden was a most unpleasant woman who ignored the fact that we had travelled a very long way, and gathered us to lecture us all on how to live in a Youth Hostel! We might not go upstairs until 8.30 p.m. – we might not take suitcases upstairs at all, but take equipment for the night by hand – we must use sheet sleeping-bags because she didn't want our germs ('bacillae') on her blankets – boys and girls must be strictly separate and no visiting allowed – we must not rise before she sang to us next morning, which would be at 6.30 a.m.! Thoroughly unpleasant atmosphere, absolutely guaranteed to wreck international relations. We went out for coffee, and, on return at 9.30 p.m., were told, when she came to unlock the door to let us in, that we ought by then to be in bed!

Sunday, 12th April: Awoke at 6.30 a.m. to 'strains' of the Dragon's singing. Breakfast should have been at 7.30 but was late. Drivers wanted to get away on time so would not allow our boys to finish washing up. But the Dragon, in her fury, impounded the luggage of Diete, our interpreter,

*Montgomeryshire County Youth Orchestra and Youth Choir at Fronhofen,
Baden Württemberg, April, 1964*

Photo: Hilda Hunter

and only let him have it on payment of 20 marks. A free fight between
the drivers and Diete on one hand, and the Dragon on the other, was
apparently only averted by Diete's calm acceptance of the situation, and
his assurance that he would be able to get his money back from the Youth
organisation who had planned our stay at this hostel. The hostel itself was
immaculate, but the atmosphere... We set off with enthusiam for Brussels.

Monday, 13th April: Up early, and after breakfast were driven to Ostend.
No more incidents, and soon we were crossing to Dover in sunshine on
a very calm sea – as different as possible from our outward journey. Were
met at Dover by coaches which took us to Folkestone for lunch, then on
to M.1 and towards home. These coaches were much less comfortable
and efficient than the 'Top Travel Tours' coaches which we had become
used to, and the journey seemed very long and tedious; the last part of it
was very uncomfortable as all the children and ourselves were crowded,
together with our luggage, into two buses which were never built to carry
so many people. What happened to the third coach we never quite knew,
except that the driver was not well, the engine kept losing water, there
was no heating on it, and breakdowns were frequent; presumably it
eventually limped home – but we would all patronise Belgian coaches in
future!

The tour had been an enormous success, principally for the experience it gave to the children in so many ways, and because of the very high quality of their musical performances. Welsh-speaking people have no word for 'playing' instruments; they speak instead of 'singing' them – 'canu'r offeryn'. Thus they encapsulate the qualities of beautiful tone and sustained melodic line which are so characteristic of their performances, whether vocal or instrumental. Even now, I still have in my head the sound of 'Calon Lân' which they sang – which we all sang – at every opportunity and with total sincerity! Here is the first verse:

> Nid wy'n gofyn bywyd moethus,
> Aur y byd na'i berlau mân;
> Gofyn'r wyf am galon hapus,
> Calon onest, calon lân.
> Calon lân yn llawn daioni,
> Tecach yw na'r lili dlos,
> Dim ond calon lân all ganu –
> Canu'r dydd a chanu'r nos.

(I do not ask for a life of luxury, worldly gold or beautiful pearls. I pray only for a heart which is honest, clean and happy – full of goodness, purer than the white lily. Then will I sing praises to the Lord, by day and by night.)

During 1964, Brodie again urged me to continue the research which I had done for my M.A. degree, and he introduced me to the Applied Psychology Department of the University of Aston in Birmingham. There, I had excellent guidance, principally from Dr. Graham Harding, and embarked upon another programme of experimentation.

I had the blessing of the Principal at Wolverhampton on my work at Aston, but I had problems in finding time for it. For a while I continued to teach in Montgomeryshire, but Peter Davies left the County to take a post elsewhere and music there lost much of its impetus. I had increasing commitments at home, and as often as possible I took my parents and Mary out in the car, to enliven their now somewhat monotonous lifestyle. I decided that it was time for me to withdraw from the County and also temporarily to curtail my research.

After Father's death in 1967, I felt that I could resume my work at Aston. Part-time research at a distance of fifteen miles from one's full-time work becomes a rather protracted affair. Eventually, in 1970, having completed my experimentation, disproved my original premise, and typed and presented my thesis, I was awarded the degree of M.Sc. in Applied Psychology by the University of Aston in Birmingham.

Meanwhile, another interesting musical activity had developed. Walter Bergmann needed assistance in teaching recorder at a Summer School organised annually by Margaret Murray in Salzburg, Austria. Margaret is an internationally famous exponent of the principles of teaching music through the integrated use of voice, untuned and tuned percussion instruments, dance and drama. The originator of specific techniques in this field was Carl Orff, of whom Margaret was a great friend. The courses which she organised were held at the Orff Institute which is a Department of the Mozarteum Academy of Music in Salzburg. She invited me to assist Walter in his Recorder teaching in the 1968 course, and additionally to give a lecture on a subject of my own choice, related to Music in Schools.

This was the first of a series of ten such visits to the Orff Institute, which I made annually from 1968 to 1977. The Courses were attended by music teachers from all corners of the globe, and one had the interesting task, when preparing a lecture, of being meticulously careful to avoid ambiguity and of ensuring that everything could be understood even by people whose acquaintance with the English language was minimal. These were most enjoyable events, wonderfully stimulating, both musically and personally. I made many new friends, for there was great rapport among Staff and Students.

I always travelled by car to Salzburg. On the occasion of my first trip, Margaret asked me if I could possibly take a young teacher with me. Though I enjoyed travelling alone, I agreed to take this teacher. She proved to be none other than my good friend Marie Isherwood from Lancashire! We had a very happy journey together, and though we had been delayed by some eight hours at Southend Airport, we had both been so keen to arrive in good time that, in the event, we arrived a whole day early!

Each year, I selected a different route and tried to include a mountain pass which I had never crossed before. I changed my car in 1973 for a Volkswagen Motor Caravan, and with that I had greater freedom to roam about in the mountains and in remote parts of Austria, Switzerland, France and Germany. I loved those journeys and the Courses which made them necessary, but sadly, due to changes in organisation, the last was held in August, 1977.

Bill Ingley and I had for some time contemplated collaboration in the writing of a book to give guidance to teachers of music in general, and to our own College teachers-in-training in particular. We set to work on the project very happily, producing a fastidiously scrutinised and checked manuscript. I had undertaken production of the book and Bill the marketing, and in 1974,

Music for Today's Children became available. A reprint soon became necessary. Profit had not been our objective, but we concluded the operation with very few copies unsold and a little cash in hand.

During the same year, Mother had her fatal heart attack and Mary was living with Doris. Doris knew that I wanted ultimately to retire to Shropshire, and in 1975 she told me that a very attractive house, just opposite to her bungalow, was becoming available and that I could buy it if I so wished. Retirement was, at most, four years distant, and despite involving myself in daily driving of eighty miles, I bought the house, believing that I could make myself available to provide care and transport for Mary, and for Doris who had by now given her car to a friend.

During the mid-70's, re-organisation of Colleges of Education was taking place. In addition, our College in Wolverhampton was threatened by the imminent continuation of the Ring Road which was planned to pass straight through its site. A great number of hours were devoted by committees of our College Staff, in collaboration with the Education Authority, to viewing alternative sites, measuring them in detail and planning their adaptation to our needs. In the event, amalgamation with existing Colleges in the University Institute of Education was regarded as the preferable option, and our building was closed in the summer of 1978. Some older members of Staff, whose retirement was imminent and of whom I was one, were offered redundancy, which we accepted. In the week following my last day at College, the building was demolished completely.

Chapter 10:

TRANSPLANTATION AND TRAVEL

A year or so before retirement from College, I had become an Examiner for Trinity College of Music, London. I travelled all over the country to examine candidates in all aspects of music studies, and I had many interesting experiences. I did tours in Scotland, where one of the Centres was situated under the shadow of Ben Nevis; and in Wales, where, on one wintry evening, having crossed the Preseli Hills, all that my hotel at Tenby could find for me to eat was baked beans on toast!

I was usually presented with a variety of instrumentalists or singers in the course of a day of examinations, at all levels from beginners to diploma standard. On one occasion I saw more than a hundred recorder players in a couple of days; and at a centre in Wales I spent two whole days examining harpists!

Festival adjudicating came my way, too, and for the most part, this was very enjoyable, though very demanding. One had to listen intently to a performance whilst simultaneously writing comments and suggestions as to how performance might be improved. Then, immediately after a series – sometimes a very long series – of performances, one had to address the audience of candidates, parents and teachers, evaluating the series of performances, announcing winners and presenting trophies. Very rarely indeed, one heard a performance which was so musically captivating that one sat back and didn't write a word!

Towards the end of 1977 I had become friendly with a doctor named Jimmy, who had been forced, by ill-health, to retire in 1972. He was very interested in music, and preferred jazz, and piano improvisation, which he could do and I could not! He had a lovely old piano, but it was incapable of remaining in tune, and he preferred to play on mine. After some time, having 'fallen' for my piano, he 'fell' for me too, and asked if he might share my home. I surprised myself by saying "Yes"! Marriage was not contemplated; Jimmy believed that marriage-vows were for life and he did not intend to abandon his existing responsibilities – a view which I respected.

Doris was initially delighted to hear our news and there were fond embraces all round. However, next day, she called on us again and announced that she had been reconsidering our position. She had decided that her principles and moral scruples would not allow her to condone our 'liaison'. Jimmy and I both said that, though we regretted her attitude, it made no difference to our decision. We would still be prepared to share the care of Mary, to give Doris some time on her own. She refused this offer, saying that she could not permit Mary to become contaminated by our immoral liaison. So Doris and Mary lived on one side of the road, and Jimmy and I lived on the other. Jimmy's friends and mine were told of our arrangement and given the option to withdraw their friendship, but the majority chose not to do so.

In October, 1978, I was invited by Trinity College to make a two-months' examining tour in Australia. I told the College that I would like to take a companion who was a doctor. They were pleased about this, because three previous examiners in Australia had contracted serious illnesses and had been involved in complex rearrangements, cancellations, and medical situations. They gave their blessing – but, naturally, no financial assistance! We flew first to Sydney, then to Brisbane, then we travelled south again by hired car. I examined at various places en route, including a Seventh Day Adventist College at Cooranbong in which we both had a wonderful welcome and where I was periodically fed, during my examining, with fruit pudding! No tea, coffee, alcohol, meat, fish, or poultry – or smoking – were allowed in the College. Back in Sydney, I was taken in a tiny plane to Bathurst, a very remote spot, then back again to Sydney. We then drove south to Kiama where the weather was impossibly hot and I had three electric fans in my small examining room to keep myself and the candidates in reasonable condition. Then we went to a little Centre at Berkeley, a very poor area, where the teacher, though not very well-off herself, gave all her lessons free of charge, arranged concerts at her own expense, and occasionally hired a bus to take her pupils to concerts in Sydney. I think that she paid their examination fees, too, and she gave a brooch to each child who was successful.

Then we flew to Wagga Wagga where the local education board – which had questionable standards in music – was cramping the style of the teachers working to achieve Trinity College levels of competence. On from Wagga Wagga to Canberra in a five-seater aeroplane of Kendall Lines. I had to sit next to the pilot, and as we flew between the hills, I was watching for potential emergency landing places in the fields beneath, as the journey was incredibly bumpy! Then I had to do a detour to a Centre at Cooma, seventy miles away, where our hostess was a charming Danish lady and hospitality was wonderful. Not only were her candidates good, but I awarded her unusually high marks in her own diploma examination. Whenever she wrote to me afterwards, she always signed herself 'Marretje 93%'!

The Australians whom we met were charming people, keen to take us around and to show us the beauty of their country.

For the concert
Of life
No~one has
A programme

A gift from Marretje van Wezel Cooma, N.S.W., Australia, 1978

From the intense heat of the Australian summer, when people wandered about in sleeveless dresses or shorts, trying but failing to keep cool, and when from the open shop doors one was bombarded by the sounds of Christmas carols – for it was only a few days to Christmas Day – we flew back to the grey chill of an English December.

A few years after the Australian adventure, I received a letter and a present of a Parker pen from a candidate in Wagga Wagga. She had taught and successfully presented some of her pupils to me for examination, but I had failed her in her own Teaching Diploma examination. She had written to me asking for advice and I had sent books and suggestions. Eventually, after a great deal of effort and careful study, she had passed her Diploma Examination. She wrote to express her gratitude to me for failing her, because she had not realised, until that time, the depth of skill and musician-ship that is required in successful teaching of music. She had since become much more competent and confident, and was altogether a happier teacher.

On 4th August, 1980, the day of the Queen Mother's eightieth birthday, Jimmy and I moved to a bungalow in Copthorne, on the west side of Shrewsbury. This was more appropriate in view of Jimmy's progressive loss of mobility. He still enjoyed travelling, and his favourite way of doing this was by motor-caravan.

We made many visits abroad, to Denmark, Germany, Switzerland and many times to various'regions of France, in which our favourite region was Alsace, where we enjoyed the interesting mixture of French and German culture. We spent most of our time touring, as increasing immobility prevented Jimmy from venturing more than a few yards from the van. I enjoyed wandering off to do shopping, and I remember seeing a postcard illustrating the song 'Ma Normandie' in a shop in Courseulles. The owner of the shop was interested that I had learnt the song at school, and he became quite animated when I joined him in singing it!

In April, 1984, we made a very memorable journey to Venice, travelling on the Orient Express in both directions. The most comfortable part of the journey was in the British Pullman between Victoria and Folkestone. The Orient Express train itself was wonderful to see, with its beautiful polished wood surfaces and elaborate marquetry, and its air of elegance and courteous service. However, comfort was at a premium, since the bench seats in our individual compartments were very narrow and hard, and so were the beds! Changing for the evening meal had to be achieved edgeways, so small was the space available! However, that was an experience never to be forgotten – though probably never to be repeated.

Venice was, at that time, the terminus for the Orient Express. It was a most fascinating, though wildly expensive, city. In St. Mark's Square, two cups of coffee without music cost 6,000 lire (£3 in 1984). If one took coffee whilst the orchestra played, two cups of coffee cost 9,000 lire (£4.50)! We visited the islands of Murano (where we saw Venetian glass being made), Burano and Torcello. At the end of our visit, we paid for all we needed before re-boarding the Orient Express and used up all our lire. Transport from our hotel was by boat, and we had reserved enough lire to tip the boatman; but we had failed to allow for the boathook man who stood on the quay, holding our boat steady whilst we disembarked. We indicated that we had no money to tip him. He became indignant and threw his cap on the quay in anger; I had to go to the Bureau de Change to get some more lire in order to placate him!

In 1985 we went to Innsbruck by train. One of the highlights was a wonderful sleigh ride through the snowy forests of nearby Seewald. When we started, rugs were taken off the horses and flung over us; when we stopped, the horses were rugged up again; and for our return journey the rugs were again transferred to us. We smelt distinctly 'horsey' on our return to our hotel!

The shop windows in Innsbruck, as elsewhere in Austria, were most artistic, as were the wrought iron signs over the doors of the shops under the arches along the pavement.

During the outward rail journey, our arrangements for help for Jimmy at all critical points had worked well, but we encountered one problem on our return journey. Innsbruck Station has an underpass and no lift. The solution devised by the officials was that Jimmy and our luggage should be loaded on to a flat luggage wagon and wheeled across the wide expanse of railway lines!

At this time, we attended many Carriage Driving Trials in England, since Jimmy had a keen interest in horses. The same procedure happened at each event – dressage, marathon and driving between cones. Our van became well-known at these events as a meeting-place for friends we had made, and for cups of coffee for all comers, at all times of day. We gradually lost interest in the events and stopped attending. However, we did go to Carriage Driving Trials in Fontainebleau, on one of our French trips. We were recognised and made very welcome by some drivers and officials whom we had met at International Trials in England.

In later years we went to watch horse-racing at Bangor-on-Dee and Ludlow, since we lived mid-way between those two racecourses, and Jimmy could watch from the van. We also visited Newbury Races several times. On one occasion, whilst I was parking the van, Jimmy had got into conversation with a man who was being treated with some deference. Someone came over and spoke to him, addressing him as 'General'. Jimmy, being interested in military matters, asked him to what his rank referred. It transpired that he was a retired General of the King's Shropshire Light Infantry Battalion. His headquarters had been the Sir John Moore Barracks, which adjoin our garden at home! We were given V.I.P. treatment, and at Jimmy's request we were introduced to Mrs. Jenny Pitman, with whom we were invited to take breakfast two days later, on our way home. Much to Jimmy's delight, she first took us out over the gallops where her horses are trained, and after breakfast she showed us round the stables and introduced us to each of the horses! We were made very welcome and spent a delightful morning before continuing on our journey.

In 1987 we returned to Venice by air and boarded the M.V. 'Orient-Express'. Our cruise took us through the Corinth Canal to Athens, where I climbed the Acropolis to the Parthenon and afterwards suffered severe sunstroke! We continued to Istanbul where a coach took us to various places of interest.

We returned to the ship and continued our voyage. We were taken to see Ephesus and its vast Amphitheatre where St. Paul preached; then we went on and visited the island of Patmos where we were taken round the monastery in which St. John the Divine wrote the Book of Revelation. Finally, we visited the stadium where the first Olympic Games were held in 776 B.C. Then we returned to Venice, and came home by air.

We went on several other cruises. The least interesting was on S.S. 'Norway' to Miami, a place we did not enjoy visiting. We also went on the Q.E.II. The weather was extremely rough when we left Southampton and few people appeared at breakfast next day. Not until several days later did we hear that she almost had a collision with a freighter in the Solent!

SOUTHERN EVENING ECHO
Friday 7th October 1988

Power of new engines ends near-miss crisis in the Solent

CAPTAIN PRAISED IN QE2 ESCAPE

THE SKILL of the QE2's Captain Alan Bennell was being applauded today after the Solent was the scene of a second major shipping near-miss in a week.

Captain Bennell's skill adverted a major incident after the 66,000 ton Cunard liner, sailing out of Southampton, was caught by a freak 72 knot gust of wind as she made a sharp turn to port off Cowes.

With the 50,000 ton container ship Benavon coming up the Solent ready to enter Southampton Water, the QE2 was sandwiched between the container vessel and the shore.

As the wind blew her towards Cowes there was a real threat she would go aground but quick thinking by Captain Bennell who lives at Bassett, Southampton saved the day. He rapidly put the massive liner astern and corrected the turn.

Captain Bennell said from the ships bridge today: "I thought we were going alongside in Cowes!

We were making the turn and, with the wind, she locked in the middle of the turn. We were unable to come round to port.

I could see she wasn't going to make the turn and when you are aware of that situation you make other arrangements.

She responded magnificently. With the new engines fitted you have immediate power at your fingertips and we were able to do eight knots astern straight away.

With the steam engines we had before the major refit we might have been a different story today."

A fisherman aboard the boat Sally Ann Jane in the Solent heard Cowes harbourmaster Captain Henry Wrigley congratulate Captain Bennell for his skillful manoeuvre which pre-

vented a potential disaster.

The fisherman, from Hythe, added: "The QE2 was no more than ship's length from going aground off Cowes harbour. She was being blown out of the main channel.

The Cowes harbourmaster came on the radio an congratulated the master of the QE2 for getting out of a very difficult problem."

Earlier this week, the tanker Polyviking ran aground on her way to Esso at Fawley with a large cargo of North Sea crude oil on board, shutting the port for more than three hours.

The QE2 was sailing for an Iberian cruise with around 1,800 passengers on board and was also battling against high winds today as she crossed the Bay of Biscay.

By courtesy of the 'Southern Evening Echo'

We visited Ibiza, Cannes, Barcelona and Gibraltar. The final visit on this cruise was to Lisbon, where we sailed up the Tagus under the impressive bridge and were taken on a tour of the city, which is full of interest.

The most interesting cruise of all was a double one, aboard the 'Sea Princess'. We went first to Huelva, then to Casablanca, after visiting which Jimmy was thrown from an electric wheelchair on which he was being returned aboard. I tried to catch him as he pitched forward on to the quay, but his momentum bowled me over and we fell in a heap. Jimmy suffered only superficial injuries, but we both felt very shocked. It was some time before he recovered some of his confidence. We continued to Tenerife, La Palma, Madeira and La Coruña, where we saw the grave of Sir John Moore, after whom the barracks at the end of our garden were named. We stayed aboard the Sea Princess for her next cruise which was to the Baltic Capitals. We visited Kristiansand, Norway; Visby in Gotland, which is Swedish; Helsinki, Finland; St. Petersburg, Russia; Stockholm, Sweden; and Copenhagen, Denmark, and we were taken by coach to see each city.

We spent one very enjoyable Christmas at Gleneagles Hotel, which Jimmy knew well, having been taken there by his mother in the 1920's, since their home was nearby. There was plenty of interest for Jimmy, and I was able to swim every day in the luxurious pool. Jimmy bought tickets for the Christmas Draw, and won first prize – a return visit for four days, with chauffeur-driven car available for the whole time! We returned in the following April, when Perthshire was looking at its best, and we enjoyed several lovely journeys in the area.

Jimmy was having increasing health problems as time went on. Gradually, our holidays became less ambitious, and though we went to France on many more occasions, we sometimes had to curtail or cancel our planned holidays for health reasons. Visits to Consultants necessarily became more frequent, and there were two emergency admissions to hospital.

On one occasion when Jimmy visited his Consultant, he was left in no doubt that a heart problem existed which might at any time prove fatal. At the end of the visit, he asked me to take him straight to the Undertaker so that he might make plans for his funeral. Details were discussed and eventually finalised to his satisfaction. His greatest concern was to ensure maximum simplicity, and the best quality of music. We then invited Bill Ingley and his wife Mary (who were in the habit of visiting us) to come and discuss Jimmy's funeral music. They had by now moved to Tewkesbury, where Bill, having studied for, and been granted, the 'Reader's Diploma under the Authority of the Archbishops of Canterbury, York and Wales' on 9th October, 1987, had become very heavily involved in the religious, as well as the musical life of the Abbey.

Jimmy and me – 1992

Bill agreed to play the organ at Jimmy's funeral, and he and Mary paid us several visits to discuss the music in detail. Jimmy wanted different harmonies for 'Brother James' Air' and together, he and Bill devised a version which satisfied them both. They compiled a service and its accompanying music, for which Bill agreed to be responsible, and Jimmy was content. He always said afterwards that nobody could have enjoyed his own funeral music as much as he had done!

Ill-health became more and more persistent and complex, until Jimmy could do very little for himself and could not be left alone at all. This continued for a period of several years. His wife had for many years been a welcome and friendly visitor at our house, and we at hers. She visited us on the afternoon of 6th September, 1995, and the three of us chatted together with great pleasure. She had just left us, and I was about to prepare Jimmy's meal, when he had a heart attack which was instantly fatal.

Bill and Mary came for several days at the time of Jimmy's funeral, in which every detail was carried out precisely in accordance with his wishes. The Minister concluded his eulogy with the words: "Jimmy will always be remembered by his former patients and friends as the 'Beloved Physician'." How very true!

Bill, Mary and I met during the following winter. The last occasion of our doing so was on a cold, snowy day just before Christmas, 1995, when we enjoyed a very cheerful meal at Much Wenlock, a part-way point between our respective homes.

Jimmy had died on 6th September, 1995, at the age of 74. Bill, with no preamble of apparent ill-health, died in exactly the same manner on 1st February, 1996, at the age of 72. Two very great characters and very great friends passed out of my life.

At the Service of Thanksgiving for the life of William Stevens Ingley (1923 to 1996), held in Tewkesbury Abbey, prayers were led by his friend, The Reverend Owain Bell – grandson of Sir Idris and Lady Bell with whom I had lived throughout my very happy first year in Aberystwyth in 1955. The last time I had seen Owain was at breakfast one day when he was visiting his grandparents; he was then about nine years old.

My house and garden had suffered some neglect during Jimmy's years of illness. I set about remedying this and re-organising both house and garden with minimum maintenance as my objective. I had wonderful help from friends of long standing, whose continuing friendship and support I value very highly indeed.

Chapter 11:

RETIREMENT AND REFLECTION

Though I 'retired' in 1978, my actual retirement cannot be said to have begun until nearly twenty years later. Perhaps a criterion for retirement is one's arrival at a point in life when one is no longer subject to a timetable other than a self-imposed one. By that standard, I am now truly 'retired'.

Reflection begins subconsciously and continues naturally at this juncture. It assumes far greater importance than planning for the future. To have opportunity to stand back and evaluate experience as it is being accumulated is a possibility; but it is not necessarily as accurate an evaluation of events in their true perspective as is reflection later in life, when major activity has ceased.

In one's eightieth year, a review of life seems to be a permissible exercise, provided that reflection is truly unprejudiced. The best one can hope to observe is the achievement of one's full potential – to have exploited one's talent as fully as possible. Yet perhaps this is for others to judge.

Hindsight shows me that the changes in occupation which I have made deliberately, during my lifetime, have consistently resulted from intellectual stagnation. In many areas of employment – in past decades, if to a lesser extent more recently – disquiet and disenchantment have been consequences of a waste of intellectual capital. Were this to have been harnessed and focussed, greater interest and will to work would have been created, and mental energy renewed and released, making further effort an attractive objective.

Certainly, I have enjoyed the musical part of my life far more than any other. It has demanded much more intense intellectual application and energy than any of my early employment ever did. No wonder that the science of music is classified as a 'discipline' and that it is as old and revered a discipline as that of medicine!

I can only hope that I may, through example and teaching, have pointed a way to others, by means of which they may have been enabled to experience fulfilment through their own musical activy, at least equal to – and perhaps greater than – my own. Stimulation and enjoyment come, not only from listening to music, but from the exploitation of sound in relation to time –

and therefrom in the creation of music. The consequent pleasure is then disseminated through performance, which itself potentiates communication with other people through the medium of music.

Some of my former students have proved themselves to be far more musically talented than I, and they have had wider opportunity to communicate through their performance. I have long since stepped aside, leaving them space for their own development and activity. I cannot be said ever to have reached the pinnacle of my profession – nor can I hope ever to do so – but the fact that at least two of my former students have done so, having overtaken and surpassed me many years ago, gives me great pleasure.

Some fifty years ago, I read a passage written in 1632 by George Herbert, a quotation from which I have retained in my mind as guidance and stimulation to my efforts, to whatever end they might be directed. On his being appointed to a new post in the Church, George Herbert decided to define the qualities of a true Pastor. He wrote:

> ". . . that I may have a Mark to aim at; which also I will set as high as I can, since he shoots higher that threatens the Moon, than he that aims at a tree."

For me, now, activity continues, but on a different level of intensity and time-scale. One is able comfortably to pace one's physical and mental output of energy with minimum pressure or stress. It is in this situation that reflection tends to take over, in preference to conscious planning for the future.

I have never been gregarious, though I enjoy the company of my close friends. Nowadays I tend to seek solitude rather than company. I find it, not only at home, in books and in my garden, but by going out from here, mainly in a westerly direction. I have a wide choice, for the hills of South Shropshire and the mountains of Wales are virtually on my doorstep. I can wander at leisure, or just 'stand and stare'. I can soon be among my beloved hills and think and reflect in peace. Perhaps it is significant that over there lies the sunset; on the other hand, I return home, looking towards the sunrise, and with pleasure anticipate the dawning of another day.

With remarkable synchronicity, the following passage was recently brought to my notice by my friend, Renée Morris Young, and a copy was kindly given to me by The Reverend Richard Birt of Weobley, Hereford. Thomas Traherne, in 1675, wrote thus:

"There is an instinct that carries us to the beginning of our lives. How do old men even dote into lavish discourses of the beginning of their lives? The delight in telling their old stories is as great to themselves as wearisome to others. Even kings themselves, would they give themselves the liberty of looking back, might enjoy their dominions with double lustre and see and feel their former sentiments, and enrich their present security with them. All a man's life put together contributes a perfection to every part of it, and the memory of things past is the most advantageous light of our present condition. Now, all these sparkles of joy, these accidents; hints of nature and little rays of wisdom meet together in humility."

"The greater part of our eternal happiness will consist in a grateful recognition, not of our joys to come, but of benefits already received."

ACKNOWLEDGEMENTS

The following have kindly given their permission for the inclusion of copyright matter in this book:

> The Birmingham Post and Mail Ltd.
> Photograph of 'The Leasowes', Halesowen.
> Birmingham University: Five Professors of Music.

> BBC Worldwide, Limited.
> Cover photograph from the Welsh Edition of 'Radio Times',
> 5th August, 1955.

> The Southern Evening Echo.
> The Q.E.II Escape – 7th October, 1988.

> Powys Cultural Development Office, Llandrindod.
> Photograph of the Mid-Wales Youth Orchestra.

> Peter Beaumont and Messrs. T. W. Howarth, Limited, London.
> Photograph of David Theodore.

> Mr. Glynn Pickford, Aberystwyth.
> Photograph taken in the National Library of Wales, Aberystwyth,
> on the occasion of the visit of Her Majesty Queen Elizabeth II.

> Mrs. Violet Davies, Aberystwyth.
> Photograph of Staff and Students of the Music Department,
> University College of Wales, Aberystwyth.
> Photograph of the author.

Although I have gone to every length possible to obtain permission for the use of all copyright material, in certain cases this has proved impossible. If this causes any problems, the persons affected should contact me.

This book has been enhanced very considerably by the generous contributions offered and made by my friend, Charles Cleall. He is responsible, not only for the Preface, but also for the meticulously compiled List of Illustrations and Index. For these, and for the unstinted encouragement with which he has supported me in my work, I am most sincerely grateful to him.

Hilda Hunter

Previous publications:

The Grammar of Music
 The Student's Music Library,
 Edited by Percy M Young,
 (Dennis Dobson, 1952)

Music for Today's Children
 W. Stevens Ingley and H. Hunter
 (H. Hunter, 1974)

Teaching the Recorder
 Series of articles first published in
 Music Teacher, Vol. 56
 (Evans Brothers Limited, 1977)

Illustrations

Index

Railway at Blackheath, 8, 21
Rally, 1937; Girl Guides', 61
Randall; Mary, 89f, 104f
Reavley; Eliza (*aunt*), 46
Reavley; Will, 46
Reddal Hill Orchestra, 75
Redruth, 96
Renshaw; Cyril J, 97
Reserved occupation, 29, 74, 82
Roads, 10
Rome, 110
Round Oak Steelworks'; 'The
 Earl of Dudley's, 10
Rowley Hill, 10
—— Rag, 10
—— Regis, 1
—— —— ; Vicar of, 27
—— —— railway station, 65
—— tunnel, 8
Rowton Castle, Shrewsbury, 29,
 118, 121f
Royal Academy of Music; The, 79
—— Artillery Band, 61
—— Normal College for the Blind,
 29, 118, 121f
—— Society of Artists' Galleries, 91
Rubbra's *The Dark Night of the
 Soul;* Dr Edmund, 109
Rüdesheim, 127
Rugby, 97
—— School, 79

Salzburg, 130
Schloss Langenburg, 126f
Scilly Isles, 95
'Sea Princess'; SS, 139
Seewald, 136
Selwyn College, Cambridge, 101
Sennen, 95
—— ; Concert at, 95
Shakespeare's plays, 27
Shaw; Dr Edmund, 21
—— ; Dr Edmund John, 21
Shenstone; William, 19
Shrewsbury, 124

Shropshire, 124f, 131
—— ; South, 144
Sidaway; Elizabeth (*aunt*), 16
—— ; Fanny (*aunt*), 5
—— ; Kezia (Mrs E J Shaw: (*aunt*),
 6, 16f, 21, 26f,
—— ; Martha (*grandmother*), 5
 death, 25
—— ; Sarah Martha (*mother:* See
 Hunter), 7f
Siloh Chapel, Aberystwyth, 102
Silver Jubilee of HM King George
 V, 8
Snow Hill railway station, 65
Solent; The, 138
Southampton, 138
Southend, 130
Spanish Civil War, 62
Staffordshire County Council
 Education Committee, 49, 83
St Andrews course, 99
St Catherine's, IOW, 95
Stewart; John Graham, 2
Stewarts & Lloyds Ltd, 2, 8, 81,
 83, 119
 treatment of veterans, 16
 dictates family-routine, 21
 Ambulance-Brigade camp, 26
 employs Doris, 28
 reserved occupation, 29, 74
 lends HH an oboe, 57
 interviews HH, 60
 employs HH, 74f
St John the Divine, 138
St Mark's, Venice, 136
Stockholm, 139
Stourbridge Concert Society
 Orchestra, 57, 74
—— High School, 32f, 49f
St Petersburg, 139
Street traders, 22
Stroud, 93
Sturman; Mr, 9
Sunbeam bicycles, 71
Sweden, 139